T·H·E Can Opener Gourmet™

T·H·E

Can Opener Gourmet™

More Than 200 Quick + Delicious Recipes Using Ingredients from Your Pantry

LAURA · KARR

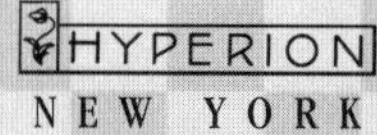

NEW YORK

Library of Congress Cataloging-in-Publication Data

Karr, Laura.
The can opener gourmet : more than 200 quick and delicious recipes using ingredients from your pantry / by Laura Karr.
p. cm.
Includes index.
ISBN 0-7868-8749-4
1. Quick and easy cookery. 2. Canned foods. I. Title.

TX833.5 K37 2002
641.5'55—dc21

2002069051

Hyperion books are available for special promotions and premiums. For details contact Hyperion Special Markets, 77 W. 66th Street, 11th Floor, New York, New York 10023, or call 212-456-0100.

Book design by Lorelle Graffeo

FIRST EDITION

10 9 8 7 6 5 4

For my grandma,

Laura Elizabeth Karr

Contents

Acknowledgments

All books are a collaborative effort, but cookbooks especially require the help of many people, and I'm going to name names. First, I want to thank my agent, Liv Blumer, for responding to the query of a complete stranger (me) and for getting this book sold so quickly. Special thanks to my editor, Jennifer Lang, for her relentless encouragement, confidence, and good cheer.

I'd also like to thank my grandma, Laura Elizabeth Karr, not only for being available at any time for quick kitchen tests and professional advice, but also for making the kitchen such a fun, loving place to be for a kid. (And thanks to my dad for taking me to visit her every weekend.)

Exponential thanks go to my intrepid home-testers, some of whom I knew and others who were recruited by friends and family. These folks bravely tasted or tested these recipes despite their busy schedules, and gave me honest feedback about both the winners and the "do-overs": Chris Agnew, Lori Aretz, Sally Bisher, Cheryl and Todd Cain, Erin Caslavka, Toni Colley, Dorothy and Rod Chronister, Cristen and Al Ferguson, Christine Hock and family, Barbara Johnson and family, Chris and Jennifer Karr, Jim Karr, Laura E. Karr, Penny Karr, Don and Tona Killingworth, Vita Patel, Scott and Sheila Petri, Julie and Kevin Reager, Michele and Brad Reager, John Redmon, Jonette Saunders and family, Carol and Harvey Snyder, Curtis Strampello, Joyce Vernoga, Marsha Vernoga, Sabine Whipple, and Eileen Workman.

For hand-holding and cheerleading above and beyond the call of duty, special thanks to Chris Agnew, Arthur E. Hilger, and Cindy Mobley. And for hand-holding, cheerleading, and occasional coaching, special thanks, too, to Neil Patel.

T·H·E
Can Opener Gourmet™

Introduction

People have asked me how I came up with the idea for this book and I tell them the truth—that I wanted a cookbook like this and couldn't find one. I'm also a little obsessed with finding the easiest, most efficient way to do things. Some might call that lazy; I call it enterprising.

And just so you understand, I'm a big fan of gourmet cooking. I love creating extravagant meals for holidays and special events. I adore big shiny cookbooks with lots of color photography showing me how to make food people will talk about weeks later. This is not one of those books. The spectacular recipes in such books are those we make when we have time—time to buy fresh ingredients, time to let things marinate and macerate, time to spend an entire day as a *sous-chef* and *saucier*. This cookbook is for the other five nights a week we eat, when we want delicious food but don't feel like running to the market or washing, chopping, and steaming. (Yet with that said, you may find recipes here that you can use to help out with your special events, such as Olive-Walnut Tapenade or Pear, Brie, and Hearts of Palm Salad.)

And I know that the emphasis in cooking today is on fresh, fresh, fresh ingredients. I thought this might be a sizable hurdle for people in considering this book. But I also thought about the fact that in television, there is something called "counterprogramming." That means that when you have a show that totally dominates a particular time slot on a particular night, you can count on the fact that there are some folks out there who aren't into it. So you put on a program that's pretty much the exact opposite in hopes of reaching them. For instance, if a sitcom about young people commands most of the viewing audience, you could probably pull in the nonconformists with a mature drama or mystery.

Well, that's kind of what I decided—that I could develop a "counter" cookbook for those days when you're not ready to go the distance in the kitchen, but don't want to resort to fast food. So I set out to create truly good food with ingredients you probably already have in your pantry.

I also tried to give a few tips along the way about using low-fat ingredients. You may note, too, that I don't use a lot of salt—I've always believed it's easier to add salt than to take it back. I also have not used any shortening or margarine in virtually any of my recipes—they have a lot of trans-fatty acids, which at this point appear to be liquid cement for your arteries. (Perhaps future generations will find the opposite is true, and that a pastry a day will keep the doctor away. But until then . . .)

Only one recipe calls for shortening and that is the 3 tablespoons in my grandmother's Maple-Buttercream Frosting. I didn't touch that. A classic is a classic.

It is my sincere hope that you'll find many dishes you can work into your weekly rotation. And I want you to feel free to experiment with the dishes—I always do. To me, a recipe is simply a jumping-off point. I also want you to feel free to substitute fresh ingredients if you like—I've given a list of equivalents so that if you have fresh ingredients on hand you may use them if you wish. After all, cooking is all about making food that tastes good to *you*.

chapter 1

Getting Started

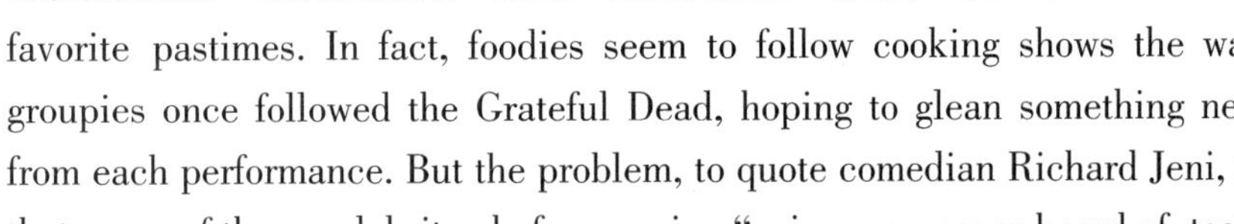

GOURMET COOKING HAS BECOME ONE OF AMERICA'S favorite pastimes. In fact, foodies seem to follow cooking shows the way groupies once followed the Grateful Dead, hoping to glean something new from each performance. But the problem, to quote comedian Richard Jeni, is that many of these celebrity chefs are using "spices you never heard of, tools you can't afford, in kitchens nicer and bigger than my house."

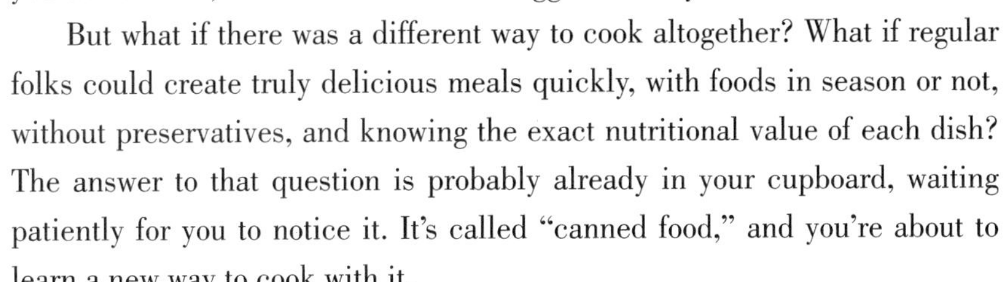

But what if there was a different way to cook altogether? What if regular folks could create truly delicious meals quickly, with foods in season or not, without preservatives, and knowing the exact nutritional value of each dish? The answer to that question is probably already in your cupboard, waiting patiently for you to notice it. It's called "canned food," and you're about to learn a new way to cook with it.

How This Got Started

THE THING IS, IT NEVER USED TO OCCUR TO ME TO USE CANNED items other than tomato sauce. Then I got married and came face-to-face with the ugly specter of preparing some kind of meal *every* night, not just for spe-

cial occasions and not just peanut butter with a side of popcorn. Suddenly, marriage made that seem wrong somehow.

After about a year I understood how being the only person in the house who can cook might work against me. Man, it was a huge pain. Not only making the food, but the monotony of thinking up something, *anything*, then shopping, chopping, cooking, and cleaning up afterwards. I began to look for easier ways to make dishes we liked. This was a challenge because both my husband and I were pretty picky eaters, despite the peanut-butter-and-popcorn confession (although the peanut is a legume and popcorn is a grain, so there you have the amino acid chain for a whole protein).

One of my hobbies had been to re-create some of the dishes we'd been served in some of our favorite fine restaurants. I was pretty good at guessing ingredients and usually had the right ones on hand or at least knew which markets might carry them. But as every cook knows, lack of ingredients is the mother of invention. For me, it was the pork loin chops with plum sauce.

I'd already set out the chops to thaw when it occurred to me that not only did I not have any plum sauce, I didn't have any plums, and they weren't even in season. And if I *could* find plums, I'd have to cook and puree them, and where did I store that silly food processor anyway?

Then I remembered something: Once I was in a grocery store with a friend who had to buy baby food for her nephew. "That vanilla pudding isn't too bad," she had said.

Momentarily horrified, I thought about it. Baby food *was* food, after all. But I had assumed that it was full of bland combinations along the lines of pureed turkey with Brussels sprouts, specially made for burgeoning baby digestive systems and their alien nutritional needs.

But I was desperate. And curious. I went to the grocery store and to my surprise found baby jars of pureed plums with apples. Checking the label for ingredients, I was shocked to learn that the only ingredients were real plums, apples, and water—no additives or preservatives. That made sense. It was for babies, after all. No one would sell chemicals to babies.

Now, I must tell you I don't have a baby and I felt pretty silly in the checkout line with all those tiny little jars. I had an excuse ready should my checker ask: I was buying the food for my niece. My alleged niece (no one asked), who ate a lot of plums.

Back home, I poured them all into a pan. Yep, the consistency was pretty good. All it needed was a little rice vinegar and, well, you can read about it in "Sauces and Dressings."

The sauce was really good. And I felt as if I had stumbled onto a great shortcut that used natural ingredients I could find any time of year. Can't say that about fresh plums.

Next, I started slipping in some canned corn here, some marinated roasted red peppers there. I used that combination on my pesto pizza . . . nobody noticed. In fact, it became an instant favorite. And before I knew it I was haunting the canned food aisles, furtively dumping in white asparagus and sliced mushrooms. Then I dipped my toe into uncharted waters—canned roast beef. I was afraid but reasoned that I had eaten beef soup, chili con carne, and beef stew from cans, so what was my problem? One Beef Stroganoff Sauvignon later and I had no problem.

Then other ideas occurred to me. We had had wonderful butternut squash soup at our favorite fine restaurant and I wanted to make it at home. But did I really want to seed, chop, boil, and puree a big ol' squash in order to make that soup? Nope.

Back at the grocery store it turned out that babies, indeed, eat butternut squash. They also eat sweet potatoes, which seemed like a good way to add sweetness without overpowering the squash. Six squash and sweet potato jars later, I had the base for my Butternut Squash and Apple Soup. Woo-hoo!

I started brainstorming about all the ways I could substitute the already cooked and pureed natural ingredients packaged in those tiny jars. One time I went to the checkout counter with about ten jars of baby food and a bottle of vodka for a marinade. Baby food and vodka—they must have thought I was the worst mother in the world!

Then the baby food idea spread to other canned items. Sweet young peas went pretty well in my Indian Samosas. Draining canned spinach made it perfect for use in my Greek Spinach and Feta Pastry or my Spinach Gnocchi.

I was giddy. Everything tasted great and it was like having my own personal *sous-chef*! (I've never been big on all the chopping and preparation that's necessary with so many recipes.) And the ingredients were suddenly available year-round. I could store them indefinitely, which cut down on my trips to the store. It also cut down on my husband's occasional sorties to find an ingredient I'd forgotten. He just didn't get the whole supermarket "endless variety" thing and would call me several times from the store so I could talk him through his mission and ensure he came back with the right stuff. An onion is not a "seen one, seen 'em all" kind of vegetable.

Anyway, it went on like that until it finally hit me: What if you could make entire *gourmet* meals using only pure ingredients stored in cans and jars? But still, it was canned. What goes into this stuff? I did some research and learned many interesting facts about canned items.

Things You Didn't Know About Canned Foods

IT TURNS OUT THAT CANNED FOODS HAVE BEEN AROUND A LONG, LONG TIME. In fact it was Napoleon, the man who said "An army marches on its stomach," who kicked off what would be the beginning of the canned food industry. In 1795 he offered 12,000 francs to anyone who could find a way to preserve food so that he could feed his military wherever they might march.

In 1809, Nicolas Appert collected the reward for his method of sealing food inside a jar or bottle, heating it, and leaving it sealed until it was ready for consumption. It would be another fifty years before Louis Pasteur found that heat killed microorganisms and the seal prevented others from invading.

The very next year, in England, tin-coated iron cans were developed (no more breakage), and this technology spread to the United States a few years later. By the end of the nineteenth century the first automatic can-making machines were introduced, and by 1955 canned foods even proved safe to eat after participating in nuclear testing in Nevada.

Besides representing the ultimate in food preservation and storage, canned foods offer some surprising health and convenience benefits.

THEY'RE GOOD FOR YOUR BODY

* Canned food (and thus your cooking) is nearly always **additive-free**. The heat process sterilizes the food and the vacuum process preserves it indefinitely, **without the use of preservatives**.
* **Baby food**, used in many of my sauces, cakes, and soups, is also virtually additive-free; it's usually just the fruit or vegetable pureed with a little water.

THEY ELIMINATE PESTICIDE RESIDUE AND OTHER PESKY VARMINTS

* Commercial canning not only destroys bacteria that cause food spoilage, but can also eliminate as much as 99 percent of the pesticide residues occasionally found in fresh produce. This is accomplished through the normal washing, peeling, blanching, and heat processing of canned fruits and vegetables.
* Canned tuna does not carry the risk of histamine poisoning, as does fresh tuna.

THEY SEAL IN NUTRITION

* Because fruits and vegetables are generally harvested at their peak and then quickly heat-sterilized and sealed, canned items do not lose their nutritional potency in the same way as many "fresh" foods that sit in warehouses, then in trucks, and then on grocery shelves. Canned foods are also preserved in their own juices, which contain much nutritive value that is often lost with many home-cooking methods.

THEIR NUTRITIONAL VALUE IS KNOWN

* Professional food processors have already calculated nutritive values for you in accordance with government requirements, making it easier for you to make health-conscious choices.

THEY'RE GOOD FOR YOUR BUSY LIFE

Canned food

* **Keeps virtually forever.**
* Is **readily available year-round,** in season or not.
* Is **already prepared for use**—chopped, diced, pureed, etc.
* Offers great **variety**—2,500 canned products are available, with 1,500 types of foods.
* Is usually (more than 90 percent of canned items) packaged in recyclable steel, with approximately 20,000 steel cans being recycled in the United States every minute. (That's not about being busy, it's just nice to know.)

So, imagine a supply run being no farther than your own pantry. Imagine a crisper *not* filled with brown goo (formerly known as carrots) because you didn't use the contents in time. Imagine being able to simply assemble and heat entire great-tasting meals.

For me, these were ideas whose time had come.

A FEW TIPS AND THE LOWDOWN ON STORAGE

After you read this section or before you go grocery shopping, you may want to see Appendix 2, "Stocking Your Pantry," beginning on page 255. You can use it as a shopping checklist if you wish, but it may also help you decide what to buy, taking into consideration your cooking and storage-space requirements.

BARGAINS

First, I want to tell you that you can find inexpensive canned food in the darnedest places. Those "everything's a dollar" stores often offer great deals. I also find bargains at drugstores and general discount stores. Just keep your eyes peeled.

DIETARY CONCERNS

Canned food is known for being high in salt, but that's not always the case. For instance, most folks are shocked to learn that tomato puree averages only 15 milligrams of sodium per ¼-cup serving. If you're concerned about your diet, read labels. There are low-salt, low-fat, and low-sugar versions of many canned foods. Just keep in mind that you may have to increase other spices or flavorings to compensate, and you'll do just fine.

EVAPORATED MILK

What is it? It's simply milk that's twice as concentrated because the moisture content has been reduced by 50 to 60 percent. It makes wonderful sauces, soups, and desserts and is an excellent substitute for half-and-half. To make milk, just combine equal parts evaporated milk and water. Never run out of milk again!

One other thing—I've seen countless cookbooks promising that if you chill evaporated milk and beat furiously, you can make whipped cream. I have tried and tried and never succeeded. Let me know if the secret is ever revealed to you.

EXPIRATION?

Expiration dates are rarely found on canned foods. Those numbers on the bottom are manufacturers' internal codes telling them when and where the foods were processed. However, many companies are now printing a "freshness/use by" date.

The general rule of thumb is this: Canned goods will remain fresh in your pantry for two years after the date of purchase. They actually have an indefinite shelf life if stored at 75°F or less. Canned food as old as one hundred years has been found in sunken ships and it was still microbiologically safe.

That doesn't mean that after several years canned goods are guaranteed to retain all their flavor, because flavor can fade over extended periods. But it does mean that they retain all their nutritional value and are perfectly safe to eat well after the two years.

STORING LEFTOVERS

If you don't use the entire contents of your can, you may cover and refrigerate the unused portion, although I strongly suggest placing the food in a storage container first to avoid the development of off flavoring. And *always* transfer tomato products to other nonmetallic containers.

SAFETY

That hissing sound? Some cans do hiss slightly when opened because they are vacuum-packed. But if a can practically explodes or spurts when opened, the food could be spoiled. Likewise, if the can is severely dented or bulging, don't buy it. When in doubt, throw it out or return it to your grocery store. Slight dents, however, are not a problem. Just use good judgment.

TOMATOES

Don't let them get too old (use within about six months). While they will keep indefinitely, they can develop a tinny taste over time. And because of the strong acid content in tomatoes (and lemons and vinegar), be aware of the type of pan you use when cooking them. Stay away from all-aluminum and pure copper pans, as they react strongly with the acid, producing a bitter aftertaste. In the case of copper, the combination can be toxic. Use nonreactive, coated, combination or stainless steel pans.

COCOA POWDER

One of the things I like about cocoa powder is that it's so versatile. You can use it to make hot cocoa or in place of baking chocolate. The powdered form is relatively inexpensive, potent, stores indefinitely, and doesn't melt on you in the summer; and when you use it with oils, you can choose a cholesterol-lowering oil such as safflower instead of getting the hydrogenated (saturated) fat of cocoa butter that normally comes in bars of baking chocolate. Remember, it's not the chocolate itself that's fatty.

EGGS, CHEESE, BUTTER, AND MILK

Did you know you can freeze each of these items? One of the advantages of freezing foods we normally think of as refrigerator perishables is that they're there when you need them, just like canned goods. Besides, you can take advantage of bulk and sale prices (one of my favorite pastimes).

Eggs cannot be frozen in their shells, however. You may freeze whites and yolks separately or together, starting them in ice-cube trays, for example, and then moving them into sealed containers. Be sure to keep track of how many you put in each parcel for measuring purposes later. *The Joy of Cooking* has a great section with specific instructions on how to package just about anything for freezing and gives guidelines for how long they can be kept. *The Egg Handling and Care Guide* (American Egg Board) says you can freeze eggs for up to a year.

Cheese is one of my favorite things to freeze, although I don't freeze it in bricks because it tends to get crumbly. Instead, I put it through my shredder. One sandwich-size Ziploc bag holds about 8 ounces of shredded cheese and is perfect for topping vegetables, salads, and pizzas or for quick snacks such as nachos or quesadillas. Cheese should be used within about six months.

Butter and milk don't need any special packaging before freezing. I like to use them within a few months, though.

SPICES

You've probably noticed that spices are very expensive. If you have absolutely none, I recommend you buy salt, pepper, garlic powder, onion powder, and cinnamon to get started. And pay attention to the garlic and onion powder—it's easy to buy garlic and onion *salt* by mistake. Not only do you add a bunch of extra salt to your dish, but some brands contain extra chemical agents.

I've also noticed that you can buy larger amounts of spices much more cheaply in your grocer's ethnic foods section.

ORGANIZATION

This one's tough, because everyone has a different amount of space in his or her kitchen and pantry. There are, however, a couple of ways you can go about organizing your shelves so that there are fewer instances of doubling, running out, or transforming your cabinet into a time capsule. Try to rotate the newest purchases to the back so the older ones get used sooner. (I know, in a perfect world . . . but do it when you can.)

I've heard of people who organize canned goods by the color of the food. They put greens, reds, yellows, etc. in separate sections.

Personally, I like to organize by category: vegetables, meats/fish, soups/chilies, fruits, and strays such as Worcestershire sauce, pickles, and hot sauce. That's not to say everything in my pantry is arranged with military precision. My cabinets are arranged more in a "close enough is good enough" style.

A Little About Me

FRANKLY, I'M LAZY. AND PICKY. AND THOSE TWO TRAITS ARE BASICALLY WHAT gave birth to this book. It's amazing how much ingenuity can be employed in the effort to avoid needless work!

I also come from a family of cooks. My great-grandma supported herself as a cook in a boardinghouse for many years. My grandma (her daughter) was a professional cook, including many years as a wedding caterer and head chef at a junior college in California. My aunt Glenda, her daughter, was also a wedding caterer.

In fact, from the earliest times I can remember, I had always "helped" in their kitchens. I loved catering weddings because I got to open gallon cans of olives or wrap hundreds of potatoes in foil for baking. And the fun of scooping out butter with an ice cream scooper! I was clearly a strange child.

But I was also struck from a young age at how my grandma could use absolutely everything. If she was peeling peaches, they were turned into pies, tarts, and jams. Even the peelings went to the mulch pile, which would fertilize the garden. And the next summer we'd eat fruits and vegetables from that garden.

If there were extra peaches, they were "put up" (canned) in beautiful old jars and stored next to the other fruits she'd put up. Other fruits—grapes, plums, cherries—were made into jams. They were lined up in the cupboard like a glass candy rainbow waiting to brighten our toast.

There was no waste and there was much improvisation in Grandma's kitchen. That's where the art is. And that's one of the things I enjoyed so much about writing this book. The challenge of adapting gourmet recipes for use with canned ingredients and making them taste great—now that's fun!

I suppose another thing I like about this cooking method is that I don't waste fruits and vegetables in the crisper the way I used to. And I also feel good about the fact that the cans get recycled and used to make other things. It's not the mulch pile, but every little bit helps the planet.

A Little About the Book

I LOVE WATCHING COOKING SHOWS AND I ADORE MANY PROFESSIONAL COOKS. But I'm heavily into convenience. One thing that used to irk me is that I had to read a recipe all the way through to see if I had not only the right ingredients and the time, but also the proper appliances and tools before I could even *think* about making it.

So in *The Can Opener Gourmet*™ I've developed a system that will allow you to assess the situation at a glance. At the beginning of each recipe, in addition to a list of ingredients there are icons indicating the degree of difficulty (one, two, or three can openers) and the tools required (from a bowl and spoon, to an electric mixer, to the occasional food processor or hand blender, etc.). This way you can tell right away if a recipe is right for your occasion or skill level.

Along the way you'll find I can't help mentioning nutrition information and sharing food prep and storage tips—or just about anything I find interesting.

You should also be aware that I've developed these recipes with maximum convenience and taste in mind, so they are all made with dried spices. But if you wish to substitute a fresh ingredient, feel free to do so (I have included a substitutions page to guide you). Just remember that dry to fresh equivalents vary, with fresh ingredients generally requiring more.

By the same token, please understand that can weights and volumes are approximate. Where I call for a 14.5-ounce can your brand may be 15 ounces. That's just fine.

Another thing I want to point out is that I give *approximate* cooking times. I do this because everybody's oven is different, and I suggest that you start checking your dish about five minutes before it's due to be finished, just to be on the safe side.

I've also had a veritable army of kitchen testers, so hopefully we have eliminated any unclear directions. As for taste, I know that when one tester says a dish has too much garlic and another tester says there's not enough in it, I've done my job. I just want to encourage you always to flavor the food so that it tastes good to you.

One last thing. If you're embarrassed about using canned items for guests, who says you have to tell? Believe me, they'll never know, because the foods are blended with other ingredients (though with the exception of spinach, in my opinion most taste just fine on their own). Just throw the cans right into your recycling bin and no one will be the wiser.

So, now that you're armed with the basics, it's time to hit the kitchen!

chapter 2

Starters

LIGHTNING-FAST ONION DIP

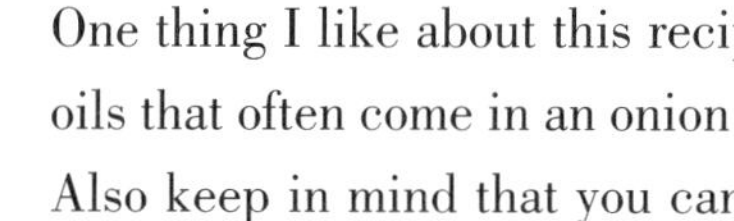

One thing I like about this recipe is that it omits the MSG and hydrogenated oils that often come in an onion dip/soup-flavoring packet. It's just plain food. Also keep in mind that you can halve this recipe if it's just for you, and you can use low- or nonfat sour cream for a lower fat, higher protein content.

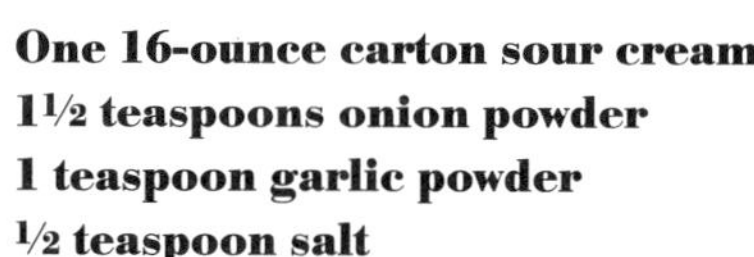

One 16-ounce carton sour cream
1½ teaspoons onion powder
1 teaspoon garlic powder
½ teaspoon salt

Mix all of the ingredients in a small bowl (or even in the carton the sour cream comes in). Serve with chips, crackers, or crudités.

Makes 2 cups

BAKED ARTICHOKE DIP

In this recipe I puree the artichokes so that I'm able to use less mayonnaise. (In fact, feel free to use low-fat mayo if you wish.) Equally at home on a holiday table or a poolside patio, this savory dip is delicious with baguette slices or your favorite crackers.

One 14.5-ounce can artichoke hearts, drained and pureed
½ cup mayonnaise
½ teaspoon bottled lemon juice
⅛ teaspoon garlic powder
Pinch salt
⅓ cup real grated Parmesan cheese (not powdered)

Preheat the oven to 350°F (unless you're planning to use a microwave oven). Drain and puree the artichoke hearts. Combine them in a small baking dish with the mayonnaise, lemon juice, garlic powder, and salt. Stir in all but 1 to 2 tablespoons of the cheese. Sprinkle the remaining cheese on top.

Bake for about 25 minutes (or microwave on medium for about 5 minutes, stirring halfway through), or until the cheese is melted and the dip is thoroughly hot.

Makes 1½ cups

BLACK BEAN AND CHEESE DIP

Black beans are high in protein and there's no fat added to them here since you mash them yourself. This is an easy starter that's both delicious and nutritious. Serve with tortilla chips and you've added a grain to complete the amino acid chain for a total protein. The dip is just great by itself, but I've listed a few other ingredients at the bottom that you may want to try as well.

One 15-ounce can black beans
½ teaspoon onion powder
⅓ cup shredded Jack cheese
Tortilla chips for dipping

Puree the beans, liquid and all, but don't overprocess. You want the dip to be just a little chunky. Place the puree in a heatproof bowl, add onion powder, sprinkle the cheese on top and heat either in a microwave on medium power or in a regular oven (set at 350°F) until the cheese has melted.

You have the option of leaving the cheese in the middle for decoration or stirring it in with the dip. Either way tastes great.

Makes about 1¼ cups.

Other ingredients you may wish to add

⅛ teaspoon ground cumin
½ cup prepared salsa
2 to 4 tablespoons canned diced green chilies
2 to 4 tablespoons bottled bacon pieces
½ cup canned diced tomatoes, drained
Mexican cheeses

SPINACH DIP

I always wondered if you could make spinach dip with canned spinach instead of frozen. I found that if you use plain yogurt instead of sour cream, something about the tartness of the yogurt keeps the spinach from overpowering the dip. The result is an enticing, piquant blend.

One 15-ounce can spinach, well drained
1 cup plain yogurt (low-fat if you're watching your fat intake)
½ cup mayonnaise (may also be low-fat)
¼ teaspoon garlic powder
¼ teaspoon onion powder
⅛ teaspoon salt

Press out as much liquid as you can from the spinach (I use a colander and press with my hands). Combine all of the ingredients in a bowl and stir well. You may serve immediately or refrigerate for later. Serve with crackers or sourdough bread.

If you do use it later and you feel the spinach taste has become too strong, just stir in a teaspoon of bottled lemon juice.

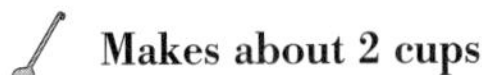

Makes about 2 cups

SALSA VERDE CLAM DIP

Before my odyssey into canned foods, I had never actually had canned seafood, except for tuna, and that not very often. Turns out I like it a lot, and I love pairing the clams and cream cheese with jalapeño peppers. Who'd have guessed?

Make sure you get the jalapeños and not just plain diced chili peppers. The jalapeños have an enjoyable tang to them.

12 ounces whipped cream cheese, at room temperature
One 7-ounce can *salsa verde* (green salsa)
1/4 cup drained, canned diced jalapeño peppers
(Use 1/2 cup if you like your dip really hot.)
Two 6.5-ounce cans chopped clams, drained (see Note)

Preheat the oven to 350°F (unless you're using a microwave oven).

Combine all of the ingredients and place them in an oven-safe or a microwave-safe dish. If you cover the dish with foil, the oven will give the edges a nice golden color, but the microwave is just fine as well. Cover and heat until thoroughly hot and bubbling at the sides. In the oven it will probably take around 20 minutes. The microwave time varies but shouldn't be more than 2 to 3 minutes on high power.

Serve with tortilla chips.

Makes about 2 cups

Note: If you want more clam taste (the peppers can overpower the clams a bit), don't drain the clams.

HOT PEANUT DIPPING SAUCE

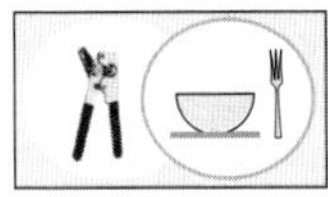

Traditional Thai peanut dipping sauce can be fairly hot, but you're in control of the heat in this recipe. The 1/8 teaspoon of cayenne pepper will yield a pretty mild sauce; 1/4 teaspoon seems about right to me. For those who like it really hot, go for the 1/2 teaspoon. Serve with a variety of raw vegetables, shrimp, or even apples. Coconut milk instead of whipping cream makes a tasty alternative, but the consistency will be much thinner.

1/4 cup creamy peanut butter (not old-fashioned or freshly ground)
1/2 cup whipping cream
1 1/2 teaspoons bottled lime juice
1 teaspoon ground coriander
1/4 teaspoon onion powder
1/8 teaspoon garlic powder
1/8–1/2 teaspoon cayenne pepper

In a small bowl, whisk together the peanut butter and cream until they are well blended and starting to thicken. Stir in the lime juice, coriander, onion powder, garlic powder, and cayenne pepper. Serve at once or chill, stirring well before serving.

Makes about 3/4 cup

MANGO SALSA WITH MINT

The mint in this recipe is optional, but try a little as a taste test. It's a really exotic combination.

You won't use all the mango, so consider using the remainder in a fruit salad, a lassi (page 242), or over ice cream.

One 15-ounce can mangoes, drained
One 16-ounce jar medium salsa
¾ teaspoon dried mint (optional)

Chop the mango into small pieces until you have half a cup's worth. Combine the mango with the salsa and mint (if using). You may serve this immediately or refrigerate it for later. I recommend letting the flavors steep a bit.

Makes about 2½ cups

VARIATION

PEACH SALSA WITH MINT

Follow the recipe for Mango Salsa with Mint, substituting canned chopped peaches for mangoes.

BLACK BEAN AND CORN SALSA

Black beans and corn not only dress up a run-of-the-mill salsa, together they supply all the amino acids of a complete protein. Unless you need to watch your sodium intake, this is a fairly healthy snack when served with baked tortillas or tortilla chips.

Prepared salsa
Canned corn, drained
Canned black beans, rinsed and drained

To each cup of salsa, add 1/4 cup each corn and black beans.

SEVICHE

Although this recipe calls for precooked tuna, seviche traditionally uses raw fish—the citric acid in the lime juice "cooks" it for you through a process of oxidation. This quick recipe makes an easy but elegant appetizer. Choose a mild to medium salsa brand you already like, or experiment a little.

One 6-ounce can tuna, drained
One 16-ounce jar salsa
1/4 cup bottled lemon juice
1/3 cup bottled lime juice
1 tablespoon oil
1 tablespoon dried cilantro
1 teaspoon sugar

Break up the tuna into small chunks or flakes. Combine all of the ingredients in a medium-sized bowl and chill for an hour or more to let the flavors blend. You can even make this the night before—time only adds to its flavor. Serve with corn chips or tortillas.

Makes about 2 1/4 cups

OLIVE-WALNUT TAPENADE

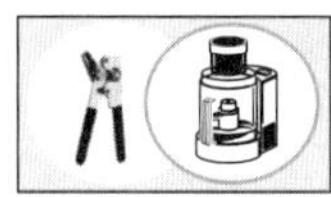

I was always wary of stuffed green olives until I finally tried them. I'm not sure what it was about them that frightened me, I'm just sorry it took me so long to give them a try. They've got a lovely tang to them that I think makes this dish, which has a strong Mediterranean feel to it.

Use this hearty tapenade as a dip or spread (it's fabulous on sourdough baguettes or toasts) or as a pesto sauce for pasta. Either way you'll get plenty of olive oil. Oh, and did I mention it was easy? Makes a quick and sophisticated party treat.

One 2-ounce jar green pimiento-stuffed olives
One 4.25-ounce can chopped black olives
1/3 cup finely chopped walnuts
3 tablespoons olive oil
2 teaspoons balsamic vinegar
1/4 teaspoon garlic powder

Drain and chop the stuffed olives until you get 3/4 cup. In a medium mixing bowl, combine the green olives with the black olives. Add the walnuts and process with a hand blender or food processor just enough to blend and smooth the nuts with the olives (you don't want a puree). Stir in the oil, vinegar, and garlic powder. The tapenade should have a coarse consistency, much like pesto.

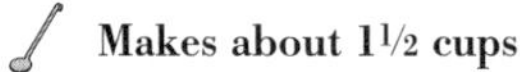

Makes about 1 1/2 cups

PARMESAN, PESTO, AND SUN-DRIED TOMATO TOASTS

Because there was so little work involved, I felt like I was cheating the first time I made these for a party. But they were a big hit and are now my "emergency" appetizers because they're easy, fast, and fail-safe.

1 to 2 baguettes (equaling about 24 inches total)
1 6- to 8-ounce jar pesto sauce
About 1 cup real grated Parmesan cheese (not powdered)
1 6- to 8-ounce jar sun-dried tomatoes

Preheat the oven to 400°F. Slice the baguette(s) into ½- to 1-inch-thick pieces. Spread a thin coating of pesto sauce onto each. Sprinkle Parmesan cheese on top of the pesto. Top with a few pieces of sun-dried tomato. Bake for 12 minutes, or until the cheese is thoroughly melted.

Makes 12 to 24, depending on how thickly the bread is sliced

HUMMUS

Pureeing a can of beans takes about 20 seconds with a hand blender, but you can also do it manually with a potato masher. Hummus is one of those healthy Mediterranean dishes we love but don't often think to make. This recipe is so simple and satisfying, you'll probably think about making it a little more often.

One 15-ounce can garbanzo beans, drained
2 teaspoons bottled lemon juice
1 tablespoon olive oil (or other vegetable oil)
½ teaspoon garlic powder
⅛ teaspoon salt
⅛ teaspoon paprika

Puree the beans. They don't have to be completely smooth; in fact, a little texture is a good thing. In a bowl, mix the pureed beans with the remaining ingredients. (If it's too thick for you, add a little extra oil or some water.) Serve with Toasted Garlic Pita Wedges (page 114).

MUSHROOM PÂTÉ

Mushrooms make a lovely pâté—the finished dish even holds its shape if you care to mold it. Serve with mild-flavored crackers or toast rounds.

One 7-ounce can sliced mushrooms, drained
2 teaspoons sherry
½ teaspoon Worcestershire sauce
½ teaspoon onion powder
⅛ teaspoon salt (optional)

Drain the mushrooms well, then puree. Add the rest of the ingredients and blend.

If using a mold, it should be about ½ cup capacity. Coat it with a nonstick spray or butter. Pack the pâté into it with a spoon, and turn it out onto a serving plate. Surround with crackers.

Makes a generous ½ cup

This recipe is easily doubled for a larger pâté.

ARTICHOKE WITH AIOLI

Aioli is basically garlic-flavored mayonnaise, but boy, what a difference some garlic and lemon make! This is a split-second starter and can be made with low-fat mayonnaise if you want to lighten it. Artichokes, of course, are low in calories.

½ cup mayonnaise
1 teaspoon bottled lemon juice
¾ teaspoon garlic powder
⅛ teaspoon salt
Two 14-ounce cans artichoke bottoms, drained
Paprika (optional)

Mix the mayonnaise, lemon juice, garlic powder, and salt in a bowl. May be served two ways: Keep the artichoke bottoms whole and spread a thin layer of aioli in their slight cups. Sprinkle with a tiny bit of paprika for color.

Or cut the artichoke bottoms in halves or fourths and arrange the pieces around a bowl for dipping. You may want to have toothpicks for easy picking and for color. You may sprinkle the aioli with a little paprika if desired.

Serves 4 to 6

GOAT CHEESE, PINE NUT, AND BACON BALL

When I first made this dish, I made 18 to 24 tiny, bite-sized balls. You can still do that, but it's a lot of work. Besides, if you make them too large, well, that's a lot of goat cheese. It becomes overpowering.

I found that making one large ball, well dredged in toasted pine nuts, and serving it with your favorite hearty crackers makes a very nice appetizer, and people can spread on as much as they want.

½ cup pine nuts
¼ teaspoon onion powder
4 ounces (½ cup) **goat cheese**
2 tablespoons bottled real bacon bits (not the crunchy kind)

Put the pine nuts in a baking pan on the top rack of the oven on low heat (about 300°F) and watch them carefully for about 5 minutes, then let cool. Pine nuts are very sensitive to heat and continue to brown and cook even after you remove them from the oven.

In a bowl, sprinkle the onion powder over the goat cheese and blend well. Add the bacon bits and blend.

Form a ball with the cheese mixture, then roll it in the toasted pine nuts, thoroughly covering it. May be served immediately or chilled for later. (It's a great make-ahead party snack.) Serve with crackers.

Serves 6

BAKED SPINACH BALLS WITH YOGURT DIP

Spinach balls may not be as pretty as some other appetizers, but what they lack in looks they more than make up for in taste. Perfect with a Mediterranean meal.

1 cup's worth canned spinach
1 cup plain bread crumbs
½ cup grated Parmesan cheese (not the powdered kind)
2 tablespoons plus 1 teaspoon lemon juice
1 large egg, slightly beaten
½ teaspoon garlic powder
¼ teaspoon salt
¼ teaspoon ground black pepper
⅛ teaspoon ground nutmeg

Yogurt Dip

½ cup plain yogurt
1 teaspoon dried dill
½ teaspoon garlic powder
¼ teaspoon salt

Preheat the oven to 400°F. Grease a cookie sheet.

Open the can of spinach over a colander and let the spinach drain, pressing to squeeze out the excess liquid. Chop well. Mix 1 cup of the spinach with the rest of the ingredients in a medium-sized bowl. Roll into 1-inch balls and place them on a greased cookie sheet. Bake for 12 minutes, or until golden-brown.

Meanwhile, make the yogurt dip by stirring together the yogurt, dill, garlic, and salt in a small bowl.

Serve the spinach balls with the yogurt dip.

Makes about 20

SWEET SPICED NUTS

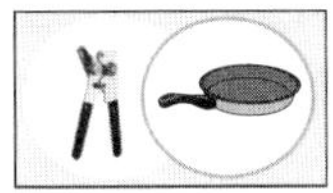

These sweet, spicy nuts make a great appetizer, especially around the holidays. They're a good snack to make when you have other things to do, since they sit in a warm oven for a couple of hours roasting away. They are also a good way to get some of your nut oils—peanut oil supplies one of the three essential fatty acids your body doesn't normally make.

One 12-ounce can salted mixed nuts
1 tablespoon oil
3 tablespoons brown sugar
½ teaspoon ground black pepper
½ teaspoon curry powder
½ teaspoon ground cinnamon
¼ teaspoon ground cloves
¼ to ½ teaspoon cayenne pepper (optional)

Preheat the oven to 275°F. Empty nuts into a large Ziploc bag. Add oil and shake and rub to coat. Combine remaining ingredients in a small bowl and whisk with a fork until smooth. Add this spice mixture to oiled nuts, then shake and rub to coat.

Spread the nuts evenly over a baking pan and roast on middle rack in the oven for about 2 hours, stirring a couple of times during baking. Toward the end of the baking process, check the nuts periodically to see if they've toasted—every oven is different.

Makes about 1½ cups

CARAMELIZED WALNUTS

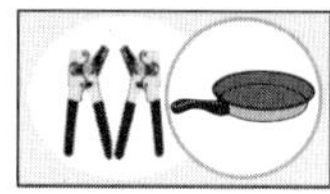

Caramelized walnuts make a sophisticated addition to salads, but they're also nice as treats around the holidays.

1 cup walnut halves or broken walnuts
½ cup sugar

Tear off about 12 inches' worth of waxed paper. Coat it with nonstick spray and set aside.

Place the walnuts in a large nonstick skillet over medium-high heat. After a few minutes they will make little crackling sounds. Continue to cook them, stirring, until they are crisp (about another 3 minutes).

At this point, sprinkle the sugar as evenly as you can over all the nuts. When the sugar begins to melt, start stirring again. The nuts are done when the sugar is completely melted and turning a nice caramel color. They turn a buttery color at first—let them go until they're caramel-colored, but not so long that they turn dark brown. You'll begin to see the contrast between the two hues after about 3 minutes.

When done, place the nuts on the coated waxed paper until cool, then serve or store in an airtight container.

Makes about 1 cup

Note: If you have any difficulty getting the caramel off your pan, simply fill it with water and set it on the stove to boil. After the sugar dissolves, you can drain it all into the sink. If there's anything left, it will come off easily with a rubber spatula.

chapter 3

Salads

SHRIMP SALAD WITH SWEET ORANGE-BASIL DRESSING

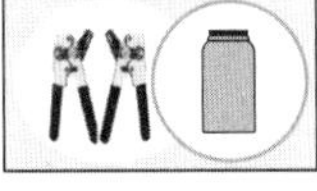

The dressing is fat free and makes enough to divide up and use for other dishes as well. This salad makes a delicious, fresh-tasting seafood treat, perfect for spring or summer entertaining. Use it as an opening course or as a main course for lunch.

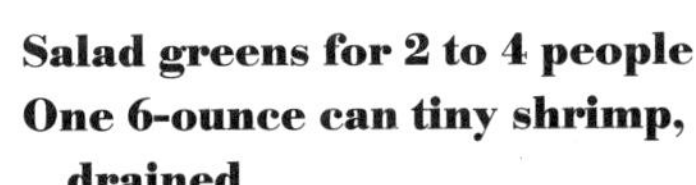

Salad greens for 2 to 4 people
One 6-ounce can tiny shrimp, drained
1 recipe Sweet Orange-Basil Salad Dressing (p. 200)
Parmesan cheese (optional)

To each plate of lettuce add ¼ can shrimp and 1 to 2 tablespoons of dressing. Sprinkle with Parmesan cheese if desired.

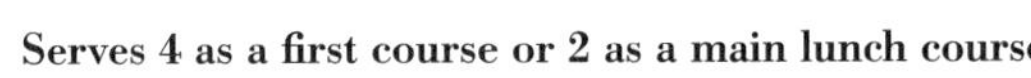

Serves 4 as a first course or 2 as a main lunch course

PINEAPPLE-BEET SALAD

Whenever I open a can of beets, I'm always amazed at how I can smell earth. It's a good, clean smell to me, reminiscent of my grandparents' garden. If you'd like a summer fruit salad that's not overly sweet, this is a good choice. Be aware that everything will turn pink when you toss the salad, so if you want to present it nicely at the table, consider forming a mound of pineapple on top of the beets first, serving individual plates at the table, and passing the dressing separately.

One 15-ounce can chunk pineapple, drained, ½ cup juice reserved
2 tablespoons olive oil
½ teaspoon sugar
½ teaspoon bottled lemon juice
¼ teaspoon salt
One 15-ounce can shoestring-cut beets, drained

To make dressing, drain the pineapple juice into a measuring cup. Combine ½ cup (or add enough water to make ½ cup) pineapple juice with the oil, sugar, lemon, and salt. Whisk to blend and slightly thicken. Combine the pineapple with the beets. Serve with dressing.

Serves 6

CHICKPEA AND ORANGE SALAD WITH LIME-MINT DRESSING

In case anyone is confused, chickpeas are also known as garbanzo beans, which is a term disliked by my spellchecker. At any rate, this is a delicious, easy-to-throw-together salad when you're craving something a little out of the ordinary.

One 15-ounce can garbanzo beans, rinsed and drained
1/4 teaspoon garlic powder
1/8 teaspoon salt
One 11-ounce can mandarin oranges, drained
1/4 cup olive oil
3 tablespoons bottled lime juice
1 teaspoon sugar
1 teaspoon dried mint
Lettuce for 4 (optional)—**consider iceberg, spinach, red leaf, or romaine**

Empty the beans into a medium-sized bowl and sprinkle with the garlic powder and salt. Stir. Add the oranges without stirring. In a separate bowl, whisk together the remaining ingredients (except the lettuce) until they're well combined. Let stand for 5 minutes, then pour the dressing over the beans and oranges, tossing gently to coat.

You may serve as is or spoon servings onto individual mounds of lettuce.

Serves 4

ANTIPASTO

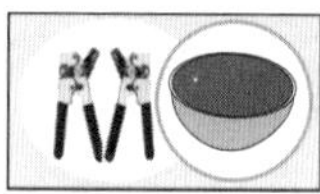

Antipasto is a simple way to add a creative touch to a meal. Serve it on lettuce as a salad, or with an assortment of cheeses, meats, hard-boiled eggs, and toast or crackers to make a first course or appetizer. It's perfectly suited for large gatherings or for giving away in decorative jars, since it makes about 2 quarts.

One 15-ounce can diced tomatoes, drained
One 15-ounce can zucchini, drained
One 15-ounce can sliced carrots, drained
One 15-ounce can small white onions, drained
One 6-ounce can large pitted whole olives, drained

Marinade

3/4 cup olive or other vegetable oil
1/4 cup apple cider vinegar
1 teaspoon dried oregano
1/2 teaspoon garlic powder
1/2 teaspoon dried basil
1/2 teaspoon sugar
1/4 teaspoon salt

You may have to drain the tomatoes more than once, as they seem to be a bottomless well. Put all of the drained vegetables into a very large mixing bowl.

In a jar or medium-sized bowl, shake or whisk together all of the marinade ingredients. Pour over the vegetables, tossing gently to coat. Then either cover the mixing bowl or spoon the vegetables into two 1-quart jars (such as old mayonnaise or pasta sauce jars) with lids. Store in the refrigerator for at least an hour before using. Storing for twenty-four hours is suggested.

Makes approximately 2 quarts

TUSCAN WHITE BEAN SALAD

White beans make a lovely salad, and you may serve this dish either warm or cold. Try serving it with a meatless pasta dish such as Tomato, Olive, and Feta Pasta (page 123), or even with some sourdough bread, and you'll balance this legume with a grain. Remember to be gentle when tossing these beans, as vigorous handling can squish them a bit. So far, my experience has been that the "small white beans" squish least.

2 tablespoons olive oil
2 teaspoons rice vinegar
1 teaspoon bottled lemon juice
½ teaspoon dried basil
¼ teaspoon garlic powder
⅛ teaspoon sugar
One 15-ounce can Great Northern, cannellini, or small white beans, rinsed and drained

Whisk together the oil, vinegar, lemon juice, basil, garlic, and sugar. Empty the rinsed, drained beans into a serving bowl and drizzle with the olive-oil mixture. Toss gently to coat. Serve as is, or heat first in a saucepan over low to medium heat until warm, or heat in the microwave on medium until warm. It will only take a few minutes.

Serves 3 (This recipe is easily doubled.)

CREAMY GREEN BEANS AND POTATOES

This dish is perfect for a summer evening. Make it ahead and serve cold or serve at room temperature right after it's made. It's also a salad that travels well. What's more, you can shear off the calories and fat by using nonfat sour cream and mayonnaise.

One 15-ounce can sliced potatoes, drained
1/4 teaspoon salt
One 15-ounce can cut green beans, drained
1/2 cup sour cream
1/4 cup mayonnaise
2 tablespoons evaporated milk
1/4 teaspoon dry mustard
1/8 teaspoon garlic powder
1/8 teaspoon sugar

Empty the potatoes into a medium-sized bowl and separate the slices if they stick together. Salt the potatoes with 1/8 teaspoon of the salt. Add the green beans and salt them with the remaining 1/8 teaspoon salt. In a small bowl, whisk together the remaining ingredients. Pour this mixture over the green beans and potatoes and toss everything to coat. Add salt and pepper if desired.

RED, WHITE, AND BLACK BEAN SALAD

This savory bean salad is sweetened and made more colorful by the presence of corn. It's terrific served hot or cold and can be made ahead of time for picnics or parties.

One 15-ounce can red kidney beans, rinsed and drained
One 15-ounce can black beans, rinsed and drained
One 15-ounce can small white beans, rinsed and drained
One 15-ounce can sweet corn, drained

Dressing

1/3 cup olive oil (or oil of choice)
1/4 cup rice vinegar
1/2 teaspoon garlic powder
1/2 teaspoon ground cumin
1/2 teaspoon ground black pepper
1/4 teaspoon chili powder
1/4 teaspoon salt
1/4 teaspoon cayenne pepper (optional)

Combine beans and corn in a medium- to large-sized mixing bowl.

To make the dressing, combine all of the remaining ingredients and either whisk in a bowl or shake in a covered jar to mix. Pour the entire contents over the beans, then toss to coat and to blend the colors.

This can be served immediately or made ahead and left to marinate in the refrigerator up to 8 hours.

Serves 8 to 10

CURRIED CHICKEN AND ARTICHOKE SALAD

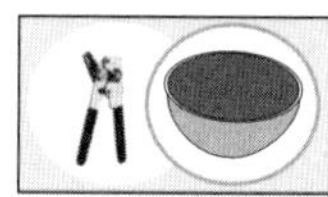

The curry in this dish brings out a sweetness you don't expect. Great as a salad or a sandwich, or consider serving scoops in canned pear halves.

One 10-ounce can chicken, drained
One 6-ounce jar marinated artichoke hearts, drained and chopped
½ cup raisins
½ cup mayonnaise
1 tablespoon rice vinegar
1 teaspoon curry powder
¼ teaspoon garlic powder
Salt (optional)
Ground black pepper (optional)

Mix all of the ingredients thoroughly. Add salt and pepper to taste and serve as desired.

Serves 4

TURKEY SALAD WITH CRANBERRY BALSAMIC VINAIGRETTE

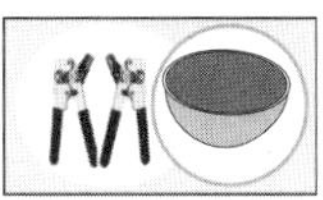

Both the salad and the vinaigrette may be made ahead and refrigerated until ready to serve. And even kids will like the cranberry dressing.

Turkey Salad

One 10-ounce can turkey, drained
Half of one 8-ounce can water chestnuts, drained and chopped
½ cup mayonnaise
½ cup raisins
1 tablespoon rice vinegar
¼ cup chopped toasted pecans (optional)

Cranberry Balsamic Vinaigrette

¾ cup salad oil
¼ cup balsamic vinegar
¼ teaspoon salt
⅛ teaspoon pepper
½ cup canned whole cranberry sauce

To make the salad, mix all of the ingredients together so that they're well coated. To toast pecans, heat in a nonstick skillet over medium heat until they begin to crackle. Or toast on a cookie sheet in a 350°F oven for about 5 minutes.

To make the vinaigrette, combine all of the ingredients and process in a blender until smooth.

Place the turkey salad on a bed of lettuce or toast, then drizzle with vinaigrette.

Serves 4

GREENS WITH TOASTED WALNUTS, BEETS, AND GORGONZOLA

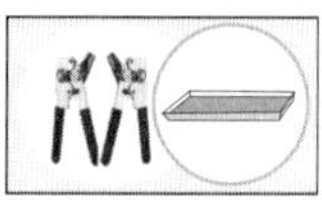

If you're not a Gorgonzola fan, consider using goat cheese or feta instead. As for the lettuce, choose something like mesclun or a "European" salad blend—something with rich dark greens and purples. If you like, you can caramelize the walnuts (see the recipe for Caramelized Walnuts on page 32) instead of toasting them. Either way is scrumptious.

1 cup broken walnuts
½ cup oil
⅓ cup balsamic vinegar
10 to 16 ounces lettuce (enough for 4 to 6 people)
One 15-ounce can sliced or julienne-cut beets, drained
4 ounces Gorgonzola, goat, or feta cheese

To toast the walnuts, place them in a large nonstick frying pan over medium-high heat and cook, stirring regularly. The oil in nuts can heat up pretty quickly, so watch them carefully. They're done when they start making a crackling sound and the edges begin to brown.

In a glass jar with a lid or other container, mix or whisk together the oil and vinegar.

Place the lettuce on individual plates. Sprinkle each with about ¼ cup of beets and about 2 tablespoons each of toasted walnuts and cheese. Add dressing as desired.

Serves 4 to 6

À SANTÉ SALAD WITH CREAMY LIME DRESSING

As many vegetarians know, combining a grain with a legume provides the complete amino acid chain normally found in a whole protein. I'd like to say I knew this a few years ago when I was craving kidney beans and corn, but I didn't. Sometimes it turns out it's just good to follow your taste buds. By the way, "à santé" means "to your health" in French.

Fresh baby spinach leaves (enough to serve 2 to 4)
½ cup canned kidney beans, rinsed and drained
½ cup canned corn, drained
¼ cup pickled beets, julienne cut, drained
2 tablespoons raw sunflower seeds
Hard-boiled egg, sliced or crumbled (optional)
Grated cheese (optional)
Peanuts (optional)
Bacon bits (optional)

Creamy Lime Dressing

3 tablespoons bottled lime juice
1 tablespoon salad oil
2 teaspoons sour cream
1 teaspoon sugar
½ teaspoon ground cumin
¼ teaspoon green Tabasco Sauce (optional)

Wash and dry the spinach and put it in a large bowl. Top with the remaining ingredients, including the optional ingredients if desired. Toss well.

Combine the dressing ingredients in a small bowl and whisk until well blended. Pour over the salad and and toss to coat.

 **Serves 2 as a meal, 4 as a starter**

PEAR, HEARTS OF PALM, AND BRIE SALAD WITH WALNUT CREAM DRESSING

Hearts of palm have an enticing taste not unlike that of artichoke, yet they're different. I love 'em.

Salad

Enough lettuce for 4 (Use a plain one such as butterhead or iceberg so it doesn't compete with the other flavors.)
4 to 8 ounces Brie, still chilled and firm (it's easier to cut this way)
One 14-ounce can hearts of palm, drained
One 15-ounce can pear halves in light syrup

Walnut Cream Dressing

1 cup heavy cream or whipping cream
¼ cup finely chopped walnuts
2 tablespoons rice vinegar
2 teaspoons horseradish

Put mounds of lettuce on individual plates. Cut 1 to 2 ounces of Brie per serving into bite-sized pieces. Sprinkle atop the lettuce. Cut stalks of palms into ¼-inch discs, about one stalk's worth per plate, and sprinkle atop the lettuce and Brie. Place one pear half on top of each salad.

In a small to medium bowl, whisk together the dressing ingredients, then drizzle over the salads.

Serves 4

CAESAR SALAD

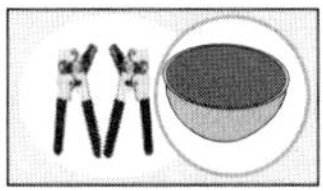

This is a salad that doesn't keep well, so you'll want to make it just before serving time. However, this version requires only minimal effort yet still captures the engaging character of Caesar salad.

One 10-ounce bag torn romaine (Should serve 4 to 6.)
½ cup olive oil
2 tablespoons bottled lemon juice
2 anchovy fillets from a 2-ounce tin, chopped fine or mashed
½ teaspoon garlic powder
¼ teaspoon dry mustard
½ cup real shredded Parmesan cheese (not powdered)
1 to 2 cups croutons (packaged or see Black Pepper Croutons recipe on page 115)

Place the salad greens in a large serving bowl. In a separate bowl, whisk together oil, lemon juice, anchovies, garlic powder, and mustard. Pour over the salad. Add the Parmesan cheese and croutons and toss everything together to coat. Serve at once.

Serves 4 to 6

CRAB SALAD WITH LEMONY VINAIGRETTE

If you're looking for a quick, delicious salad without any leftovers, this is the one. Since crab is a mild shellfish, choose a lettuce that's mild as well, such as iceberg or butterhead. This recipe can easily be doubled, tripled, etc.

One 6.5-ounce can crab, drained and flaked, cartilage (if any) **removed**
2 tablespoons mayonnaise
3/4 teaspoon Homemade Seafood Spice (page 89)
1/2 teaspoon bottled lemon juice
Lettuce for 2 salad servings
Sliced almonds for sprinkling (optional)

Vinaigrette

1/4 cup olive oil
1 1/2 tablespoons rice vinegar
1/2 tablespoon bottled lemon juice
1/8 teaspoon mustard powder
1/8 teaspoon garlic powder
1/8 teaspoon onion powder

In a small mixing bowl, combine the crab, mayonnaise, seafood spice, and lemon juice. Place a serving of lettuce on each of two bowls or plates, and scoop half the crab mixture on top of each. Sprinkle with sliced almonds if desired (they add a nice crunch).

To make the vinaigrette, combine all of the ingredients in a lidded glass jar or a bowl. Shake or whisk together briskly.

Pour the dressing over the crab salads.

Serves 2

SMOKED OYSTER AND POTATO SALAD WITH LEMON VINAIGRETTE

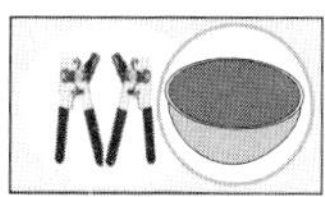

This is a versatile dish—serve it over arugula as a salad or on good-sized sourdough toasts as an appetizer. You could even serve it alone as a potato salad. Oysters tend to come in different sizes, so simply cut them (they slice easily) if they're too big for delicate, bite-sized pieces. Likewise, the potatoes will crumble easily enough when stirred if they're too large for polite bites.

One 8-ounce can water chestnuts
½ teaspoon (or more) **celery salt**
One 15-ounce can sliced potatoes, drained
One 3.75-ounce tin smoked oysters, rinsed and drained

Vinaigrette

½ cup salad oil
2 tablespoons bottled lemon juice
½ teaspoon sugar
⅛ teaspoon onion powder
⅛ teaspoon garlic powder
⅛ teaspoon salt
¼ teaspoon dried parsley
Arugula (optional)
Toasted sourdough rounds (optional)

Drain and dice the water chestnuts. Put them in a mixing bowl, sprinkle them liberally with celery salt, and stir. (You will need a little over half a teaspoon or more—taste it to decide.) Mix in the potatoes and oysters.

To prepare the vinaigrette, combine all of the ingredients except the parsley in a bowl or lidded jar. Whisk or shake until well blended. Pour about half the vinaigrette over the potato-oyster mixture and toss to coat. (Save the rest, if desired, for another salad.) Sprinkle with the parsley flakes. Serve as is or scoop onto arugula or your choice of lettuce, or mound onto slices of sourdough toast sliced as thickly as you desire. You'll need about 4 slices.

Serves 4 generously as an appetizer or 2 as a good-sized salad

SALADE NIÇOISE

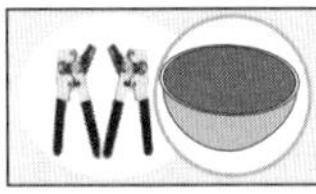

Niçoise means "as prepared in Nice," and dishes prepared in this fashion generally include black olives, garlic, anchovies, and tomato. Salade Niçoise usually includes the above plus green beans, potatoes, tuna, hard-boiled eggs, onions, and herbs. All in all, it makes a pretty hearty salad, fit for a starter or a main course. Consider serving it with whole-wheat crackers and chilled white wine.

Salad

4 eggs (If you don't wish to use eggs, consider substituting about 1/2 cup real grated Parmesan cheese—it's not traditional but it sure tastes good.)
1 bag mesclun or European-blend salad serving at least 4 (A head of red lettuce works as well.)
One 15-ounce can sliced potatoes, rinsed and drained (see Note)
One 14.5-ounce can cut green beans, drained
One 2.25-ounce can sliced or one 6-ounce can whole black olives (Kalamata or Niçoise olives are fine, too.)
One 12-ounce can chunk white albacore tuna, drained
4 to 6 anchovy fillets (one for each person)**, chopped fine** (optional)
One 15-ounce can diced tomatoes, drained (optional)

Niçoise Vinaigrette with Lemon

1 cup olive oil
1/3 cup rice vinegar
1 tablespoon bottled lemon juice
1/2 teaspoon dry mustard powder
1/2 teaspoon garlic powder
1/2 teaspoon onion powder

Place the eggs in a medium-sized saucepan and cover with water. Bring to a rapid boil, then turn the heat down to low and cook for 10 to 12 minutes. Remove from the heat, drain, and and fill the pan with cold water to stop them from cooking. After the eggs have cooled, peel and chop.

In a large mixing bowl, combine the lettuce, potatoes, green beans, about half of the olives, tuna, anchovies, and tomatoes, if desired.

To make the vinaigrette, whisk together all of the ingredients until the dressing begins to thicken. Pour about three-quarters of the dressing over the tuna mixture and toss to coat. (Or serve on individual plates of lettuce and let your guests dress and toss their own.)

Bring the remaining dressing and olives to the table for further garnishing.

 Serves 4 to 6

Note: Be sure to rinse the potatoes in a colander, as they have starch on them. It doesn't taste bad, it's just an incongruous texture for the salad.

WHITE BEAN, OLIVE, AND SUN-DRIED TOMATO–TUNA SALAD

This full-bodied salad offers the benefits of fish oil, olive oil, and fiber. I've used small white beans here; you may use cannellini or Great Northern beans, but I find the small white beans hold up better (less squish factor). Feel free to use more tuna if you're looking for extra protein. Also, I like to pour some plain vinegar directly on the salad, even with the dressing. I've been told I like too much vinegar, but it's an option for you if you'd like.

One 6-ounce can tuna, drained
One 3.8-ounce can sliced black olives, drained
One 15-ounce can small white beans, rinsed and drained
2/3 cup drained, chopped sun-dried tomatoes from a jar
1 teaspoon onion powder
1/8 teaspoon celery salt
1/4 cup olive oil
1/4 cup rice vinegar
Enough of your favorite lettuce for 4 main courses or 8 starters
Parmesan or feta cheese (optional)
Walnuts, chopped fine (optional)

In a medium-sized mixing bowl, combine the tuna, olives, beans, and tomatoes. Sprinkle with onion powder and celery salt, then toss.

In a small cup, whisk together the oil and vinegar. Pour about half of the dressing over the tuna-bean mixture and toss gently to coat. Serve on mounds of lettuce. Sprinkle with as much cheese, walnuts, and more dressing as desired.

Serves 8 as a starter or 4 as a main course

chapter
4

Soups

CREAM OF ASPARAGUS SOUP

Each can of asparagus contains only about 60 calories, and if you use nonfat evaporated milk, you're going to get an elegant, low-fat soup that's perfect for a first course. The evaporated milk really comes through with a creamlike taste. I served this at a holiday dinner and didn't tell anyone where I got the asparagus when they complimented me on the soup.

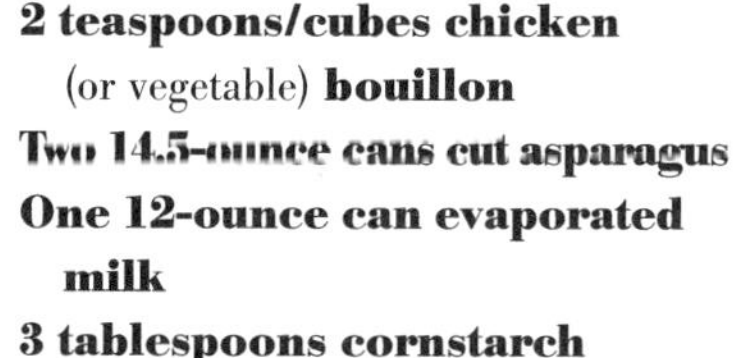

2 teaspoons/cubes chicken (or vegetable) **bouillon**
Two 14.5-ounce cans cut asparagus
One 12-ounce can evaporated milk
3 tablespoons cornstarch dissolved in a little cold water, just to make it smooth

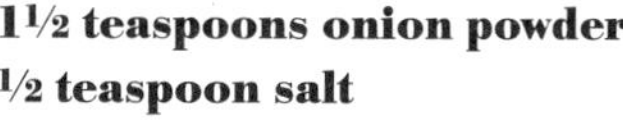

1½ teaspoons onion powder
½ teaspoon salt
¼ teaspoon garlic powder
¼ teaspoon bottled lemon juice
Salt (optional)
Ground black pepper (optional)

In a medium saucepan, combine the bouillon with 2 cups of water and set over medium-high heat to dissolve. Meanwhile, drain and puree both cans of asparagus pieces.

When the bouillon has dissolved, stir in the pureed asparagus, milk, and cornstarch. Blend in the onion powder, salt, garlic powder, and lemon juice. Bring to a low boil and stir until thickened. Add salt and pepper if desired.

Serves 6

BUTTERNUT SQUASH AND APPLE SOUP

This is one of my favorites, both because it tastes great and because it was my first soup creation using baby food. You might not want to tell folks right off how you got your butternut squash puree. They'll never guess.

Five 4-ounce jars butternut squash baby food
One 4-ounce jar sweet potato baby food
One 15-ounce can chicken broth
½ cup unsweetened applesauce
¾ teaspoon onion powder
¼ teaspoon ground nutmeg
⅛ teaspoon ground pepper (white or black)
Crème fraîche for garnish (optional)

Combine all of the ingredients except the crème fraîche in a medium-sized saucepan. Cook over medium heat, stirring. You may also heat this in a microwave, but I just find it tastes better when pan-heated. When the soup is just beginning to boil or is steaming, remove it from the heat.

For the optional garnish, if you don't have a pastry bag or cake-decorating kit or you don't feel like cleaning said kits, cut a *tiny* piece (like 1/16 inch) off a bottom corner of a regular Baggie. Put a tablespoon or so of crème fraîche into that corner without squeezing.

Crabbing above the cream, tighten the bag around the cream with one hand and squeeze it out with the other. You can make concentric circles and draw diagonal lines across them for a varied look.

 **Serves 4**

CREAM OF RED BELL PEPPER SOUP

My favorite restaurant makes a delicious red bell pepper soup. The first time I had it, I knew I had to go home to the "lab" and figure out how to make it—the easy way, of course. I was pleasantly surprised at how true the flavor was and how easily it came together.

I use a hand blender for most of my pureeing needs. If you don't have one or a food processor, use your blender and just keep mashing down the peppers.

One 24-ounce jar marinated red peppers, drained
One 12-ounce can evaporated milk
One 14-ounce can chicken broth
1 tablespoon cornstarch (optional)
Pinch cayenne pepper (optional)

Puree the drained peppers until they have a consistency like applesauce. I like the tiny bits of red in the soup—I think they give it a little body and character. But if you like a true puree, blend away.

Pour the pureed peppers into a medium-sized saucepan. Add the milk and chicken broth and cook, stirring, over medium-high heat until the soup begins to simmer. You may serve the soup now, or you may wish to bring its consistency to that of a chowder.

If you would like a chowdery soup (which I prefer), add the cornstarch dissolved in a little cold water and stir for a few minutes more, until the soup has thickened to the desired texture. Add cayenne pepper if desired.

Serves 6

CREAM OF GINGER-CARROT SOUP

I don't usually like cooked carrots, but I like this soup. It's wonderful served hot on a cold winter night or cold as a summer appetizer. The little bit of vinegar combines with the ginger to give it a subtle, citrusy flavor.

Six 4-ounce jars carrot baby food
One 12-ounce can evaporated milk
1 teaspoon ground ginger
1 teaspoon rice vinegar

Combine the carrot and milk in a saucepan over medium heat. Add the ginger and vinegar, stirring to make sure the ginger is thoroughly dissolved.

After a few minutes of stirring and heating, the soup should be hot enough for serving. If serving cold, chill in the refrigerator.

Serves 4

CHEESE BISQUE

I *love* cheese, and this is a hearty, easy soup that satisfies my addiction. It's wonderful as a meal with buttered sourdough bread and a side of cottage cheese if you want to add protein. If you want to dress up the dish a little, add the optional beer or wine for a richer note. Be sure not to use low-fat milk or cheese, or you'll run the risk of them separating or curdling.

One 14.5-ounce can chicken broth
One 12-ounce can evaporated milk
1½ cups shredded Cheddar cheese
½ teaspoon salt
Ground black pepper (optional)
¼ cup beer or dry white wine (optional)

Combine all of the ingredients in a saucepan and bring to a boil. Turn down the heat and simmer until all of the cheese has blended into the soup. Serve hot.

Serves 4

CORN CHOWDER

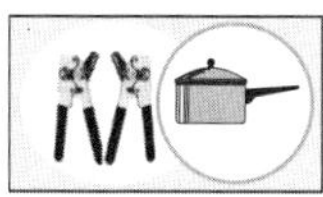

This chowder is a hearty one and is a wonderfully fast way to warm up on a cold evening after work. The soup can be made thicker by adding cornstarch, but you may prefer it as is.

Two 15-ounce cans cream-style corn
One 12-ounce can evaporated milk
1 tablespoon onion powder
¼ teaspoon salt
¼ teaspoon ground black pepper
2 tablespoons sherry or dry white wine (optional)
1 to 2 tablespoons cornstarch dissolved in a little cold water

Place all of the ingredients but the cornstarch into a medium-sized saucepan. Add 1½ cups of water and place over medium-high heat. Stir occasionally to keep the mixture from burning on the bottom. When the soup is steaming or just coming to a boil, you may either serve or add the dissolved cornstarch.

After adding the cornstarch, bring the soup to a low boil, stirring occasionally until it has thickened.

Serves 6

VARIATIONS

CHICKEN-CORN CHOWDER

To the above recipe, add one 10-ounce can of chicken, drained.

CORN CHOWDER WITH ROASTED RED PEPPERS

To the above recipe, add 3/4 cup drained and chopped roasted red peppers from a jar.

CLAM CHOWDER

All you need are a few cans and some spices to create a hearty and delicious homemade clam chowder. And you'll know everything it contains because you made it yourself. Consider serving this with Seasoned Oyster Crackers (page 120) and Caesar Salad (page 45).

One 12-ounce can evaporated milk plus 12 ounces (1½ cups) **water; or just use 3 cups of milk**
1 tablespoon butter
One 16-ounce can sliced potatoes, drained
1 teaspoon bottled real bacon pieces
1½ teaspoons onion powder
¾ teaspoon salt
½ teaspoon celery salt
¼ teaspoon ground black pepper
¼ teaspoon garlic powder
¼ teaspoon Worcestershire sauce
3 tablespoons cornstarch dissolved in a little cold water
Two 6.5-ounce cans clams, *not* drained

In a medium-sized saucepan, combine the milk, water (if using), and butter. Cook over medium heat, stirring so that the milk doesn't stick.

Chop the potatoes into small, bite-sized pieces, then combine with the milk mixture. Add the bacon pieces, onion powder, salt, celery salt, pepper, garlic powder, and Worcestershire sauce.

When the butter has melted, add the cornstarch and bring to a low boil. After the soup thickens, stir in the clams, liquid and all. Cook just long enough to heat the clams (about a minute). Serve immediately.

Serves 5

CRAB BISQUE

This is a super-easy way to make a rich crab bisque. Serve it as a first course for a special meal, or just have it yourself for lunch.

One 10.75-ounce can condensed cream of celery soup
One 12-ounce can evaporated milk
One 6-ounce can crab, drained and flaked (remove cartilage if any)
1/4 teaspoon garlic powder
1/8 teaspoon ground black pepper

Put all of the ingredients in a saucepan and stir over medium heat. Bring to a boil and serve.

If you wish to make it a smoother bisque, puree the ingredients together before heating.

BLACK BEAN SOUP WITH CUMIN AND TOMATO

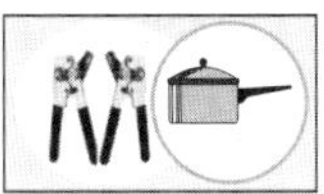

There is virtually no fat in this soup—none at all if you elect to forgo the ham. This soup can stand alone as a meal if made with ham, or as a superb side dish or first course for a Southwestern-themed meal. Consider serving it with corn bread or polenta to add a grain to the legumes and thereby complete the protein.

2 teaspoons or cubes chicken or vegetable bouillon
Four 15-ounce cans black beans, drained
One 14-ounce can diced tomatoes, drained
2 teaspoons onion powder
1 teaspoon ground cumin
¼ teaspoon garlic powder
¼ teaspoon cayenne pepper
One 5-ounce can ham, drained and diced (optional)
Sour cream for garnish (optional)

Pour 2 cups of water into a medium to large saucepan. Add the bouillon and cook over medium heat to dissolve. Puree all but ½ cup of the beans and add to the broth. Add the whole beans and remaining ingredients except for sour cream, stirring until the puree is absorbed. Heat to desired serving temperature and serve. Top with a dollop of sour cream, if desired.

Serves 8

ITALIAN-STYLE TOMATO SOUP

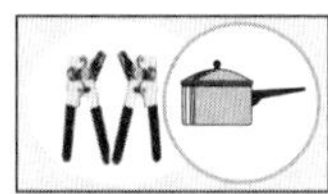

This dish can be made with or without the pasta, depending on your mood or time considerations. Either way, it makes a flavorful side or first-course dish.

I don't know about you, but I always feel guilty about wasting tomato paste—I rarely see a recipe that requires more than about 2 tablespoons of the stuff. But if you want to use it, consider cooking up a red pasta sauce and making an Italian-themed meal.

1 cup pasta shells or macaroni noodles (optional)
2 teaspoons or cubes beef bouillon
One 29-ounce can tomato puree
2 tablespoons tomato paste
1 teaspoon onion powder
½ teaspoon garlic powder
½ teaspoon dried basil
½ teaspoon dried oregano
½ teaspoon sugar
Dried parsley for garnish (optional)

If you're adding the pasta, cook it according to the package directions, then drain.

Pour 4 cups of water into a large nonreactive saucepan (meaning not aluminum—use stainless steel or a nonstick surface). Add the bouillon and cook over medium-high heat. When the bouillon is dissolved, add the remaining ingredients (except the pasta) and stir until combined. When the soup is nice and hot (just beginning to boil), add the pasta if you wish, then serve. You may want to garnish with a bit of dried parsley in the center of each bowl of soup.

Serves 8

AVGOLEMONO—GREEK LEMON SOUP

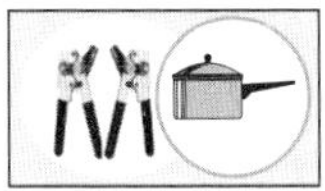

I absolutely love Greek food. I was so happy to find that this soup, often served as an appetizer, was easy to adapt. I hope it becomes one of your favorites, too. It's a great accompaniment to chicken.

½ cup rice, uncooked
6 teaspoons or cubes chicken bouillon
3 eggs
2 tablespoons bottled lemon juice
1 tablespoon butter
⅛ teaspoon salt (optional)
Dried mint leaves for garnish (optional)

Cook the rice according to the package directions. (This takes about 15 minutes.)

Pour 6 cups of water into a medium-sized saucepan. Add the bouillon and heat. In a medium-sized bowl, lightly beat the eggs and lemon juice until frothy. After the broth comes to a boil, take it off the burner. The broth should be hot but not boiling by the time you combine it with the egg. To do so, add about a cup's worth of broth slowly to the eggs, stirring, to raise the eggs' temperature. Then slowly stir the egg/broth mixture back into the soup. Add the rice and butter, stirring until the butter is dissolved. (If necessary, put the pot back on the fire.)

If desired, sprinkle dried crushed mint leaves in the center of each bowl of soup.

Serves 6

ITALIAN BEAN SOUP

Tear off a piece of sourdough bread and pour a splash of Chianti to accompany this soup. Great as a first-course dinner dish or as part of lunch.

½ cup small pasta, such as small shells or salad macaroni
4 teaspoons or cubes chicken bouillon
3 tablespoons bottled real bacon pieces (not the crunchy kind)
½ teaspoon garlic powder
½ teaspoon dried parsley
½ teaspoon dried basil
½ teaspoon onion powder
¼ teaspoon celery salt
¼ teaspoon salt
¼ teaspoon ground black pepper (optional)
One 15-ounce can kidney beans, rinsed and drained
One 14.5-ounce can diced tomatoes, drained

Cook the pasta according to the package directions, adding about ½ teaspoon of salt to the water. (You can start cooking the pasta and the soup simultaneously. When the pasta is almost done, remove it from the heat and just let it sit in the water for a few minutes to keep it warm and moist.)

Pour 4 cups of water into a large saucepan. Add the bouillon and bring to a boil. As the water heats and the bouillon dissolves, add the bacon pieces, garlic powder, parsley, basil, onion powder, celery salt, salt, and pepper. When the water begins to boil, add the kidney beans, tomatoes, and drained pasta. Simmer gently for about 5 minutes. Serve.

Serves 6

Meat and Poultry

BEEF-PINEAPPLE TERIYAKI

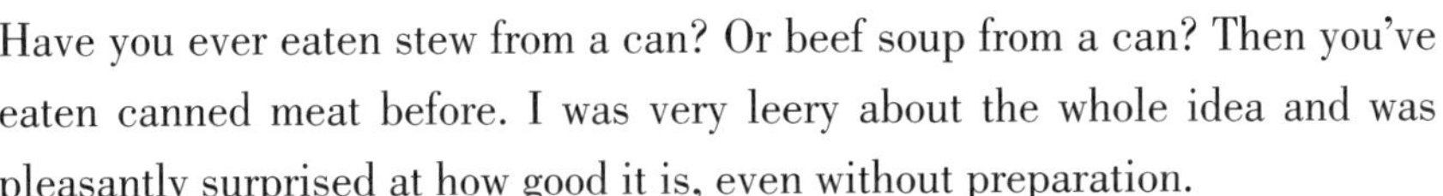

Have you ever eaten stew from a can? Or beef soup from a can? Then you've eaten canned meat before. I was very leery about the whole idea and was pleasantly surprised at how good it is, even without preparation.

As several cultures know, pineapple is a delightful way to liven up many meats. This recipe offers a simple way to add some spice to an ordinary beef dinner.

1 cup long-grain rice
One 20-ounce can chunk pineapple
1/4 cup soy sauce
1/3 cup brown sugar
1 1/2 teaspoons ground ginger
1 teaspoon dry mustard
1/2 teaspoon garlic powder

2 tablespoons sherry
1 tablespoon butter
Two 12-ounce cans roast beef, rinsed and drained
4 tablespoons cornstarch

Cook the rice according to the package directions. Meanwhile, drain the pineapple juice from the can into a measuring cup, then add enough water to make 1 cup of liquid. Set the pineapple chunks aside. Combine the pineapple juice with the soy sauce, brown sugar, ginger, mustard powder, garlic powder, sherry, and 2 cups of water; stir. Set aside.

Melt the butter in a large saucepan. Add the pineapple chunks and sauté for several minutes, until the fruit is warm and begins to brown slightly. Add the pineapple–soy sauce mixture and the roast beef chunks.

Bring to a boil, then reduce the heat and simmer for about 10 minutes. Dissolve the cornstarch in a little cold water and add to the mixture, stirring until it thickens into a sauce. Spoon over rice and serve.

BEEF STROGANOFF SAUVIGNON

This dish is typically served over egg noodles; however, I eat it with spinach fettuccine (the green ones).

One 12-ounce package egg noodles or noodles of your choice
Two 12-ounce cans roast beef, *not* drained
One 10.75-ounce can condensed cream of mushroom soup
One 7-ounce can sliced mushrooms, drained
1/3 cup Cabernet Sauvignon (or any dry red wine you have on hand)
1/4 teaspoon onion powder
1/4 teaspoon garlic powder
1/2 cup sour cream or plain yogurt (Nonfat is okay.)

Cook the noodles according to the package directions.

In a medium to large saucepan, combine the remaining ingredients except the sour cream. Heat until bubbly, then simmer for about 5 minutes. Add the sour cream or yogurt. Simmer for another 2 minutes—enough to thoroughly blend and warm the sour cream.

Salt and pepper if desired, but taste it first—you may find it just fine as is. Serve over the noodles of your choice.

Serves 6

NO-COOK-NOODLE LASAGNA

If you've ever made lasagna before, you know that part of the challenge is in working with wet noodles. Not only do you have to take the time to cook them and then let them cool so that they don't burn your fingers, you also have to fish them out and layer them without tearing them—not an easy feat.

This recipe eliminates that whole cooking and working with wet noodles step through the generous use of sauce. You get to use uncooked (stiff) lasagna noodles, which makes the job easier and faster. And I've used tomato puree instead of sauce, bringing the sodium content down. (Store-bought spaghetti sauce is usually loaded with salt.)

Of course, you don't have to make your own sauce. I've given you the option of using store-bought spaghetti sauce or whipping up a homemade one that's tasty, hearty, and simple.

One last thing—the leftovers freeze well in plastic wrap covered by aluminum foil. I wrap and freeze individual servings for quick meals.

1 pound ground hamburger (optional)
2 jars (about 32 ounces each) **spaghetti sauce**
or, for homemade sauce:
- **Two 28-ounce cans tomato puree**
- **One 28-ounce can diced tomatoes, *not* drained**
- **1 teaspoon garlic powder**
- **½ teaspoon onion powder**
- **½ teaspoon salt**
- **½ teaspoon sugar**
- **1 teaspoon dried basil**

Filling

32 ounces ricotta cheese
¾ cup real grated Parmesan or Romano cheese (not powdered)
2 eggs
¼ teaspoon salt

16 ounces uncooked lasagna noodles (about 12 noodles)
2 cups shredded mozzarella cheese

To Make Homemade Sauce:

If you're making your own sauce and you're using meat, salt the hamburger and brown it in a large saucepan, breaking it into bits. Add the remaining ingredients for homemade sauce. Bring to a boil, then lower the heat and simmer, stirring for about 5 minutes.

To Make Lasagna:

Preheat the oven to 375°F. In a large bowl, combine the ricotta, Parmesan or Romano cheese, eggs, and salt. In a lasagna pan, spread 1½ to 2 cups of sauce (enough to cover the bottom). Place four uncooked noodles on top of the sauce. Cover the noodles with 1 cup of sauce and then half of the ricotta mixture. Sprinkle ½ cup of mozzarella over the ricotta layer, then cover with 1 cup of sauce. Top with four more uncooked noodles, covering them with 1 cup of sauce. Spread on the remaining ricotta mixture, sprinkle with ½ cup of mozzarella, then cover with 1 cup of sauce. Place the four remaining uncooked noodles on top, then cover with 1 last cup or cup and a half of sauce (to cover). You may serve the remaining sauce over the lasagna at serving time.

Cover the pan with foil and bake for 1 hour. Remove the foil and sprinkle the remaining mozzarella over the top. Bake, uncovered, for 10 more minutes, until the cheese gets nice and bubbly. Take it out and let it stand for 10 minutes before serving so that the cheese is no longer like molten lava.

Serves 8

CHICKEN PICCATA

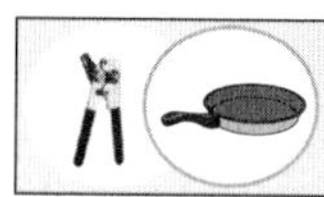

This is so easy I'm embarrassed to call it a "recipe," but it makes a nice, sophisticated main course.

4 boneless, skinless chicken breasts
Salt
Ground black pepper
3 tablespoons butter or oil (give or take, for sautéing)
3 tablespoons bottled lemon juice
½ teaspoon garlic powder
One 7-ounce can sliced mushrooms, drained (4 ounces net weight) (optional)
2 tablespoons capers, drained

Salt and pepper the chicken breasts to taste. Sauté the breasts in the butter or oil, lemon juice, garlic powder, and mushrooms (if using) until brown. The chicken is done when it is no longer pink and the juices run clear when pierced.

After the chicken is thoroughly cooked, remove it from the heat.

Place the chicken on plates with the mushrooms and cooking juices, then sprinkle a few capers (about ½ tablespoon) over the top of each. Serve immediately.

Serves 4

PENNE WITH CHICKEN, PINE NUTS, AND TOMATO

This is one of my favorites. It's hearty, with a sweet, savory tomato flavor, yet doesn't contain a lot of fat. It may quickly became a regular addition to your cooking repertoire.

12 ounces dry penne
(or similar tube pasta)
1/3 cup pine nuts
2 tablespoons olive oil
One 28-ounce can crushed tomatoes
1 teaspoon garlic powder
1 teaspoon dried basil
3/4 teaspoon salt
1/4 teaspoon sugar
One 10-ounce can chicken, rinsed and drained
1/2 cup Parmesan cheese

Cook the pasta according to the package directions.

While you're waiting for the water to boil, you can toast the pine nuts. Place them in a shallow pan on the top rack of an oven set at 350°F. Roast for several minutes. (You have to watch carefully to make sure they don't burn, keeping in mind that they continue to cook after you pull them out.) You could also put them in a toaster oven set on medium. When finished, the nuts should be golden-brown, with a few deep brown nuts. Let them cool.

In a medium saucepan, combine the olive oil, tomatoes, garlic powder, basil, salt, and sugar. Bring to a low boil, stirring periodically. Add the chicken, stir, and let simmer for at least 5 minutes (a little longer is even better—you may want to start the sauce before you start the pasta).

Toss the pasta with the sauce. Add the Parmesan cheese and toasted pine nuts, tossing again to distribute. Serve immediately.

Serves 4 to 6

BOW-TIE PASTA WITH PESTO CHICKEN AND WALNUTS

Farfalle (or bow-tie pasta) always struck me as having a certain charm, and it lends itself well to this particular dish. You can easily serve it to vegetarians if you leave out the chicken.

12 ounces bow-tie (farfalle) pasta
One 10-ounce can chicken (drained)
One 8- to 10-ounce jar pesto sauce
½ cup chopped walnuts

Cook the pasta according to the package directions.

Place the chicken in a large bowl and, using forks, pull it apart into bite-sized pieces. While the pasta is still warm, add it to the chicken and toss thoroughly. Add the pesto sauce and toss to coat. Add the walnuts and toss once more. (If you have folks who don't like walnuts, you may serve them separately in a bowl, to be sprinkled on as you would Parmesan cheese.)

Though this dish is easier to toss when warm, it may be served cold as well.

Serves 6

SPANISH RICE WITH MEAT OR POULTRY

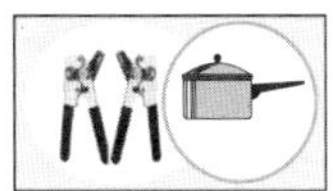

Spanish rice can make a zesty little main dish when served with meat or poultry. This is an easy recipe in which the rice does not need to be precooked. Try serving it with a green salad and corn pudding.

One 15-ounce can tomato sauce
One 14.5-ounce can diced tomatoes, *not* drained
One 4-ounce can diced green chilies, drained
1 tablespoon onion powder
½ teaspoon ground cumin
½ teaspoon sugar
¼ teaspoon garlic powder
¼ teaspoon dried oregano
¼ teaspoon salt
1 pound cooked ground beef or one 12-ounce can roast beef, rinsed, drained, and pulled into smaller bites, or one 10-ounce can chicken or turkey, drained and pulled into smaller bites
Cayenne pepper (optional)
¼ cup sliced black or green Spanish olives (optional)
1 cup uncooked medium- to long-grain rice

In a large saucepan, combine all of the ingredients but the rice. Heat over medium-high heat until the mixture just begins to boil. Stir in the rice and cover. Reduce the heat and let simmer for 15 to 20 minutes, or until the rice is tender.

Serves 6

GREEK GARLIC CHICKEN

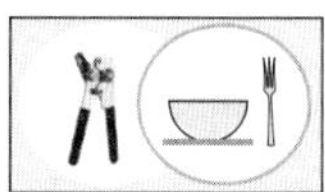

This highly flavored oil is something you can easily brush on chicken while barbecuing, baking, or sautéing. It's also wonderful with lamb. These dishes are especially good served with lemon rice and hummus.

¼ cup olive oil
2 teaspoons bottled lemon juice
1 teaspoon garlic powder
4 to 6 chicken pieces

Combine the oil, lemon juice, and garlic powder and whisk together. The garlic will tend to fall to the bottom but will be picked up by your brush or baster.

To barbecue or bake, brush the oil on liberally, reapplying during the cooking process. To sauté, pour the flavored oil into the frying pan and cook as you would normally. The chicken is done when it is no longer pink and the juices run clear.

Serves 4 to 6

CHICKEN BREASTS WITH OLIVE-RAISIN-WINE SAUCE

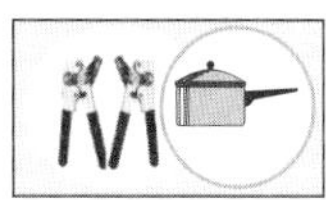

This delicious, aromatic sauce is perfect when you're looking for something new to do with chicken breasts. It's great on pork and lamb, too. You may want to serve this with black beans and rice to give it a Cuban flair.

Enough butter for sautéing
4 chicken breasts (about 2 tablespoons)
4 boneless, skinless chicken breasts
1 cup canned chicken broth or ½ cup chicken bouillon plus ½ cup water
½ cup dry red wine or ⅓ cup chicken broth plus 2 tablespoons balsamic vinegar
2 tablespoons olive oil
One 4.25-ounce can chopped black olives, drained
½ cup currants or chopped raisins
½ teaspoon garlic powder
½ teaspoon dried marjoram
¼ teaspoon onion powder
1 tablespoon cornstarch dissolved in cold water

Cook the chicken breasts as you like them. I've suggested sautéing here, since it's easy. Melt 2 tablespoons of butter in a skillet on medium heat. Brown the chicken breasts, making sure they're cooked all the way through. (They're done when the juices run clear and no pink remains.)

In a saucepan, combine the remaining ingredients except the cornstarch. Bring to a boil, then reduce the heat and simmer for about 5 minutes.

Pour the dissolved cornstarch into the hot broth mixture. Cook for another 2 minutes or so, stirring, until it has thickened enough to make a sauce. Spoon over the chicken breasts.

Serves 4

TERIYAKI CHICKEN AND VEGETABLE RICE

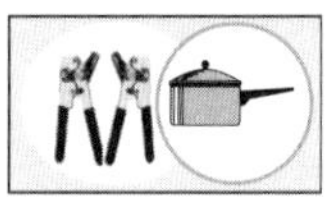

If you'd like less salt in this dish, try lower-salt teriyaki sauce and chicken broth. If you do, you may need to add a little more flavoring, perhaps with a low-sodium soy sauce.

One 14-ounce can chicken broth plus 1/4 cup water
1 cup rice
One 10-ounce can chicken, rinsed and drained
1/4 cup teriyaki sauce mixed with 2 tablespoons water
One 8-ounce can water chestnuts, drained and chopped
One 8-ounce can sweet young peas, drained
One 8-ounce can sliced carrots, drained

Bring the chicken broth and water to a boil, then add the rice. Cook according to the package directions.

Meanwhile, put the chicken in a medium to large mixing bowl and pull it apart (with forks) into bite-sized chunks. Add the teriyaki sauce plus water and stir well. Add the water chestnuts, peas, and carrots; toss with the chicken.

When the rice is done, add it to the chicken and vegetable mixture and toss well.

The dish will be pretty hot with the just-cooked rice, but if you wait to serve it, you may want to reheat it briefly first.

Serves 6

CHICKEN CURRY

Since this curry is made with only 1 tablespoon of oil, it's a low-fat yet flavorful way to eat chicken. It's also embarrassingly simple.

2 cups Curry Sauce (page 180)
Two 6-ounce cans or one 10- to 12-ounce can chicken, rinsed and drained
1 cup dried basmati (or other long-grain white) **rice**

Make the curry sauce. Stir in the rinsed, drained chicken. Let simmer for at least 5 minutes. You may let it simmer to keep warm while you make the rice—it's a good way to let the flavors steep into the meat.

Cook the rice according to the package directions. It should be finished in 15 to 20 minutes.

Serve the warm chicken curry over rice.

Serves 4 to 6

TURKEY TETRAZZINI

This dish is a great way to get some turkey into your diet. It's surprisingly elegant, too.

8 ounces dry spaghetti (or other long thin noodle such as linguine or spaghettini)
One 12-ounce can evaporated milk
One 10.75-ounce can condensed cream of mushroom soup
One 7-ounce can sliced mushrooms, *not* drained (net weight 4 ounces)
One 10-ounce can chunk turkey, *not* drained
1/4 cup dry white wine or sherry (optional)
1 tablespoon onion powder
1/4 teaspoon garlic powder
1/2 cup freshly grated real Parmesan cheese (not the powdery kind)
One 8-ounce can new peas, drained (about 3/4 cup)
1/4 cup bread crumbs
Salt and pepper to taste (optional)

Cook the pasta according to the package directions; drain. Place the pasta in a lightly greased or nonstick-sprayed casserole dish.

Preheat the oven to 375°F.

In a medium-sized saucepan, combine the milk, mushroom soup, and mushrooms (with liquid) over medium heat. When thoroughly blended, add the turkey, wine, if using, onion powder, garlic powder, and 1/4 cup of the Parmesan cheese. Stir until everything is blended and the cheese has melted. Remove from the heat and gently stir in the peas.

Pour the mixture over the noodles in the casserole dish, then gently toss to coat. Mix the bread crumbs with the remaining 1/4 cup of Parmesan cheese and sprinkle over the top.

Bake for about 30 minutes. When it is done, the top should be crisp, with bubbling around the edges.

Serves 4 to 6

VARIATIONS

CHICKEN TETRAZZINI

Follow the directions above, substituting one 10-ounce can of chicken for the turkey.

HAM TETRAZZINI

Follow the directions above, substituting two 5-ounce cans of ham for the turkey.

CHICKEN TACOS WITH MANGO SALSA

This is a great dish for those wanting to cut down on red meat. It's also a great way to cook without heating the house, since the chicken is heated in a microwave oven.

One 10-ounce can white meat chicken, drained
1/4 teaspoon onion powder
1/4 teaspoon garlic powder
1/4 teaspoon ground cumin
1/4 teaspoon coriander
1/4 teaspoon chili powder
1/8 teaspoon salt
6 taco shells or tortillas
Shredded lettuce
Shredded cheese
Mango salsa (prepared, or see the recipe for Mango Salsa with Mint, page 21)
Canned diced tomatoes (optional)

In a medium bowl, mix the chicken with the spices and salt. Heat in a microwave on high until it reaches the desired temperature (try 1 minute first).

Warm the shells or tortillas per the package directions. Fill each shell or tortilla with several spoonfuls of seasoned chicken. Add some lettuce and cheese, then top with mango salsa. (If you want to use tomatoes, canned diced tomatoes work well, but with the mango salsa you don't really need them.)

Serves 6

PENNE WITH HAM, ASPARAGUS, AND LEMON CREAM SAUCE

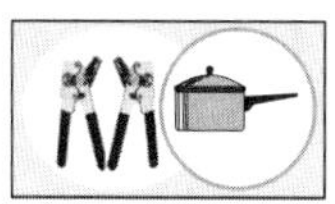

The addition of ham to the asparagus and lemon cream sauce makes this a heartier dish, suitable for a main course.

12 ounces penne (or other tube-shaped pasta)
4 tablespoons butter (½ stick)
One 14-ounce can chicken broth
One 12-ounce can evaporated milk
Two tablespoons bottled lemon juice
1 teaspoon garlic powder
½ teaspoon salt
½ teaspoon dried parsley
3 tablespoons cornstarch, dissolved in a little cold water
Salt and pepper to taste
One 5-ounce can or ¼ of a 16-ounce can of ham, drained and diced
One 15-ounce can of cut asparagus spears, completely drained
Real grated Parmesan cheese (not powdered) **for garnish** (optional)

Make the pasta according to the package directions.

Melt the butter in a medium-sized saucepan. Stir in the broth and milk. Add the lemon juice, garlic powder, salt, and parsley. When it's hot enough that little bubbles begin to form on top (or it's just beginning to boil), add the dissolved cornstarch. Stir and cook a minute or two longer, until the sauce has thickened. (If it doesn't seem thick enough, add one more tablespoon of cornstarch dissolved in a little cold water.) Stir in the ham.

Because the asparagus will break up into the sauce if too vigorously tossed, you'll want to spoon the ham and cream sauce over the pasta first, then sprinkle the asparagus over the top. You may want to have grated Parmesan cheese at the table for sprinkling.

Serves 6

FETTUCCINE CARBONARA

When I was in Rome, I tried this dish and fell in love with it. If you find yourself hankering for some and you don't have bacon, real bacon pieces from a bottle make a good pinch hitter. I've also substituted evaporated milk for the whipping cream; I find that the eggs thicken the cream sauce just fine without whipping cream, though you may use that if you wish.

16 ounces fettuccine
1/3 cup (6 tablespoons or 3/4 stick) **butter**
3/4 cup grated real Parmesan cheese (not powdered)
3/4 cup (6 ounces) **evaporated milk**
3 eggs
3/4 teaspoon salt
1/4 teaspoon garlic powder
1/8 teaspoon ground nutmeg
One 2-ounce bottle real bacon pieces (low-fat is fine)
2 teaspoons dried parsley

Cook the fettuccine according to the package directions. (You may want to start the sauce after your noodles have reached a boil.)

Melt the butter in a medium-sized saucepan over medium heat. Add the Parmesan cheese and stir until melted. Add the milk, stirring constantly (whisks are great for this), and bring to a low boil. Place the eggs in a small bowl and lightly beat them with a fork. Stir in a small amount of the hot cheese sauce, just to warm up the eggs. Slowly pour the eggs back into the cheese sauce, whisking as you do. Cook over low-medium heat, stirring, until thoroughly heated and blended (about 5 minutes). Stir in the salt, garlic powder, and nutmeg. Toss the sauce with the pasta, then add the bacon and parsley and toss again. Serve immediately.

Here's an alternate cooking method if you're nervous about curdling the eggs: Lightly beat the eggs, then whisk them together with the milk in a medium saucepan. Cut the butter into six slices, add to the milk, and cook over medium heat, stirring briskly to keep the eggs blended with the milk. When the butter has melted and the sauce comes to a low boil, add the Parmesan cheese and stir until melted. Stir in the salt, garlic powder, and nutmeg. Toss with the pasta, then add the bacon and parsley and toss again. Serve immediately.

Serves 8

GREEN BEAN, HAM, AND MUSHROOM CASSEROLE

This is a fast, creamy variation on an old favorite. Plus you get your meat and vegetables in the same dish. Use low-fat soup and milk to cut calories and fat if you wish.

One 10.75-ounce can condensed cream of mushroom soup
½ cup evaporated or whole milk
⅛ teaspoon salt
⅛ teaspoon onion powder
⅛ teaspoon garlic powder
⅛ teaspoon ground black pepper
Two 14.5-ounce cans French-style green beans, drained
One 5-ounce can ham, drained and diced
One 7-ounce can sliced mushrooms, drained (net weight 4 ounces)
¼ cup plain bread crumbs
¼ cup grated real Parmesan cheese (not powdered)

Preheat the oven to 400°F.

In an 8×8-inch baking dish, combine the soup and milk. Stir in the salt, onion powder, garlic powder, and pepper. Add the green beans, ham, and mushrooms. Combine the bread crumbs with the Parmesan cheese and sprinkle over the top. Bake for 20 minutes, or until all is hot and the topping begins to crisp.

Serves 6

chapter 6

Fish and Seafood

CLAMS NEWBURG

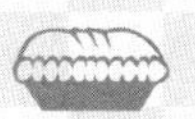

Any sort of seafood "Newburg" is a rich blend of butter, cream, egg yolks, spices, and sherry. Here I've used cornstarch with evaporated milk, which, due to its more concentrated nature, works beautifully and with substantially less fat. (Heavy cream has about 50 calories per tablespoon; evaporated whole milk has about 20. It also contains more protein.) The clams are added last so that their consistency remains tender.

One more thing I want to point out. Classically, a white sauce base is made by melting butter, stirring in flour to make a roux, then slowly adding cream or milk, whisking continually to blend them. After heating this mixture, if egg yolks are to be used, they are carefully added by combining a little hot liquid with them to bring up their temperature, and then adding them to the sauce (or worse, composing the whole thing over a double-boiler). The danger

is that if the yolks aren't warm enough when they go in, they'll curdle. If they get too warm before they go in, they'll curdle.

After so many years of cooking, I finally wondered why I couldn't combine the egg yolks with the cold milk or cream first. I called Grandma, my professional adviser. Sure enough, she had been doing it this way for years because she had to cater large events quickly. The trick is to whip the egg yolks vigorously into the cold milk so that they're combined, then heat the mixture. (Kind of wish I'd paid more attention in chemistry. . . .)

Serve this delicacy over buttered toast points. (Remove the crusts from the bread and make two opposing diagonal slices to make four triangles from a slice.) Or serve over rice if you prefer.

One 12-ounce can evaporated milk
2 egg yolks
1 tablespoon cornstarch
2 tablespoons sherry
½ teaspoon salt
Pinch cayenne pepper
⅛ teaspoon ground nutmeg
1 tablespoon butter
One 6.5-ounce can minced clams, drained
Toast or rice as desired for 4

In a medium saucepan, combine the milk and egg yolks with an electric hand blender or beater, or whisk furiously. It takes only a few seconds. Add the cornstarch and beat again to make sure it's completely dissolved. Add the sherry, salt, cayenne, nutmeg, and butter. Place the mixture on the stove over medium heat and stir until the butter has melted and the sauce has thickened.

Stir in the clams and cook for another minute or so, just to bring them up to temperature. Serve immediately over toast points or rice.

Serves 4

PASTA WITH RED CLAM SAUCE

The secret here is to add the clams last so that they don't get overcooked, which can produce extra-chewy clams. Consider serving with Baked Rosemary Loaves (page 112).

16 ounces pasta, such as linguine, spaghetti, or spaghettini
One 28-ounce can crushed tomatoes
1 tablespoon olive oil
1/4 cup dry red wine
3 canned anchovy fillets, drained and chopped fine
2 tablespoons canned tomato paste
2 teaspoons dried basil
1 1/2 teaspoons onion powder
1/2 teaspoon garlic powder
1/4 teaspoon red pepper flakes
1/2 teaspoon sugar
1/8 teaspoon salt
Two 6.5-ounce cans chopped clams, *not* drained

Cook the pasta according to the package directions.

Heat the tomatoes, oil, wine, anchovies, and tomato paste in a medium saucepan. When hot, stir in the basil, onion powder, garlic powder, red pepper flakes, sugar, and salt. Bring to a low boil and simmer for about 3 minutes. Add the clams, juice and all. Cook for another minute to warm up the clams, then remove from the heat.

In a large bowl, pour the clam sauce over the pasta, then toss to coat. Serve immediately.

Serves 8

PASTA WITH WHITE CLAM SAUCE

Again, the secret here is to add the clams last so that they don't get overcooked. Consider serving this dish with Lemon-Garlic Toast (page 113).

8 ounces pasta (half a 16-ounce package), **such as linguine, spaghetti, or spaghettini**
2 tablespoons butter
1/4 cup olive oil
1/4 cup dry white wine, such as Chardonnay
1 1/2 teaspoons garlic powder
1 teaspoon salt
1 teaspoon dried parsley
1/2 teaspoon dried thyme
1/4 teaspoon dried basil
Two 6.5-ounce cans chopped clams, *not* drained

Cook the pasta according to the package directions.

Melt the butter in a medium saucepan over medium heat. Add the oil, wine, garlic powder, salt, parsley, thyme, and basil, stirring well. Increase the heat a little and cook until the mixture begins to boil and is thoroughly heated (about 3 minutes). Add the clams, liquid and all. Stir and cook about a minute more, just to warm up the clams without overcooking them.

In a large bowl pour the clam sauce over the pasta, then toss to coat. Serve immediately.

Serves 4

BAKED CRAB CAKES

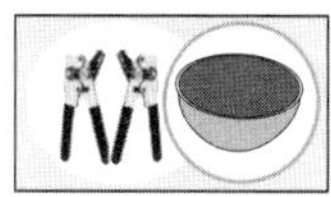

In this recipe I call for a little homemade spice mix. Don't worry—it's made of very common spices and flavorings. I had been trying to make a Cajun spice, but the result ended up being a terrific way to flavor crab cakes. Save the rest of the spice mix for other seafood dishes (such as crab salad).

Homemade Seafood Spice

1 tablespoon garlic powder
1 tablespoon onion powder
1 teaspoon white pepper
1 teaspoon black pepper
1 teaspoon paprika
1 teaspoon chili powder
¼ to ½ teaspoon cayenne pepper
¼ teaspoon unsweetened cocoa powder
¼ teaspoon sugar

Combine ingredients.

Crab Cakes

1 tablespoon melted butter
Two 6-ounce cans crab, drained, cartilage (if any) **removed**
2 teaspoons bottled lemon juice
½ cup plain bread crumbs
1 teaspoon Homemade Seafood Spice
1 egg

Preheat the oven to 375°F.

In a medium-sized bowl, mix the melted butter, crab, lemon juice, ¼ cup of the bread crumbs, and the Seafood Spice. In a separate small bowl, lightly beat the egg, using a fork, then add to the crab mixture. Stir gently until thoroughly combined.

With your hands, make six silver-dollar-sized patties. Dredge each of them in the remaining ¼ cup of bread crumbs so that they're covered. Bake on a lightly greased baking sheet for about 30 minutes, or until they're turning golden-brown and are slightly crispy on the outside.

Serves 6

CRAB-STUFFED SHELLS WITH PARMESAN CREAM SAUCE

Because crab has such a mild flavor, I needed to make sure it didn't get lost. Both the ricotta filling and the sauce are therefore subtle, just there to enhance. Originally, I filled manicotti with the crab mix, and you still may if you want, but the large shells are easier to manage and work well with a nautical theme.

12 ounces large pasta shells or manicotti tubes

Two 6-ounce cans crab, drained, cartilage removed if necessary

Filling

One 32-ounce carton ricotta cheese (not low-fat, as it doesn't hold together well)
¼ cup real shredded Parmesan cheese (not powdered)
2 eggs, lightly beaten
1 teaspoon garlic powder
⅛ teaspoon salt

Parmesan Cream Sauce

2 tablespoons cornstarch
One 12-ounce can evaporated milk
2 tablespoons butter
⅛ teaspoon ground nutmeg
¼ cup plus 2 tablespoons real shredded Parmesan cheese (not powdered)

Make the pasta according to the package directions.

In a large mixing bowl, combine the filling ingredients and stir well.

Lightly coat with nonstick spray or lightly oil a 13×9-inch or 14×10-inch dish or pan. With a spoon, stuff the shells with the crab mixture and place them in the pan.

Preheat the oven to 400°F.

In a medium saucepan, briskly whisk together the cornstarch and milk until the cornstarch dissolves. Stir in ½ cup of water, add the butter, and cook over medium-high heat. When the butter is melted, add the nutmeg and ¼ cup of the Parmesan, stirring until the cheese has completely melted. Cook and stir until the sauce has thickened (just a few minutes).

Pour the hot sauce over the stuffed shells in the pan. Sprinkle the tops with the remaining 2 tablespoons of Parmesan cheese and cover with foil. Bake until the dish is thoroughly heated, the cheese has melted, and bits of golden-brown begin to appear around the edges, about 25 minutes.

Serves 6

ANGEL HAIR PASTA WITH SHRIMP AND LEMON CREAM SAUCE

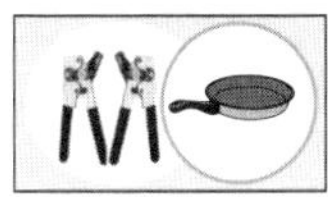

I admit I was dubious about this because I'm very picky about my seafood. But even on the first try I knew I had a keeper. One thing to bear in mind with the shrimp: Too much stirring causes them to break into pieces, so I suggest you spoon them onto the pasta and sauce before serving, or add them to the sauce just at the end.

12 ounces angel hair or cappellini pasta
4 tablespoons butter (1/2 stick)
One 14-ounce can chicken broth
One 12-ounce can evaporated milk
2 tablespoons bottled lemon juice
1/4 teaspoon garlic powder
1/2 teaspoon dried parsley
3 tablespoons cornstarch dissolved in a little cold water
Salt to taste (Try 1/8 to 1/4 teaspoon.)
Two 4-ounce cans medium shrimp, drained

Make the pasta according to the package directions.

Melt the butter in a large frying pan over medium heat. Stir in the broth, milk, lemon juice, garlic powder, and parsley. When the mixture is hot enough that little bubbles begin to form on top around the edges, add the dissolved cornstarch. Stir and cook a couple of minutes longer, until the sauce has thickened. Add salt if using.

Spoon the shrimp and cream sauce over individual plates of pasta and serve. Or slip the shrimp into the sauce just before serving.

Serves 6

SHRIMP IN SWEET ORANGE-BASIL SAUCE

You can use either tiny shrimp or the medium-sized kind for this dish. Add the shrimp to the sauce, or warm them and place them on top of the sauce on a bed of rice. The sweet-and-tart flavor of the orange juice is a delightful base for the shrimp.

1 cup uncooked rice
1 teaspoon or cube chicken bouillon
One 8-ounce box, bottle, or can orange juice
1 tablespoon sherry
1 teaspoon sugar
½ teaspoon dried basil
3 tablespoons cornstarch dissolved in a little cold water
Two 6-ounce cans shrimp, drained

Make the rice according to the package directions.

In a medium saucepan, heat 1¾ cups water and the bouillon until the bouillon dissolves. Add the orange juice, sherry, sugar, and basil. Bring to a boil, then add the cornstarch dissolved in water and stir over medium heat until thickened. Add the shrimp if you wish and heat for another minute or so—just enough to heat the shrimp. Otherwise, serve the shrimp over the sauce.

Serve warm over rice.

Serves 6

SHRIMP CURRY

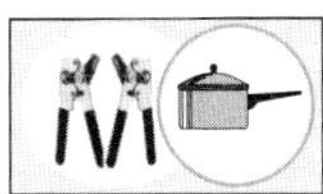

Putting shrimp in this curry makes the dish seem a little exotic, yet it's extremely simple. It's great when you get a yen for Indian food or just want a low-fat way to eat shrimp—this curry has only 1 tablespoon of oil in it. The rest is simply rigorously spiced tomato sauce.

2½ cups Curry Sauce (page 180)
1 cup dried basmati (or other long-grain white) **rice**
Two 6-ounce cans medium-sized deveined shrimp, drained

Make the curry sauce. You may let it simmer on low heat to keep warm while you make the rice.

Make the rice according to the package directions. It should be finished in 15 to 20 minutes.

When ready to serve, dish out approximately ½ cup of rice on each of four plates. Divide the shrimp between the four and place on top of the rice. Cover with ⅓ to ½ cup of curry sauce.

Serves 4

FUSILLI WITH TUNA AND LEMON

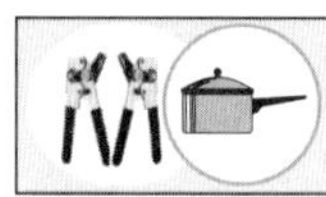

Fusilli is the little corkscrew pasta. If you don't have it, you can substitute just about any pasta in a pinch, with the exception of long noodles. If you've seen the recipe for Angel Hair Pasta with Shrimp and Lemon Cream Sauce (page 93), you'll probably notice that this recipe calls for twice as much lemon juice and makes less sauce. The reason for this is that this sauce must stand up to the strong flavor of tuna, and it should be more like a coating than a gravy.

12 ounce package fusilli
4 tablespoons butter (½ stick)
¼ cup bottled lemon juice
¼ teaspoon garlic powder
One 12-ounce can evaporated milk
¼ teaspoon salt
¼ teaspoon ground black pepper
1 tablespoon cornstarch dissolved in a little cold water
One 6-ounce can chunk tuna in oil, preferably albacore (If using tuna in water, drain it and drizzle a little olive oil over it before using.)
½ teaspoon dried parsley

Make the pasta according to the package directions and drain.

Melt the butter in a medium-sized saucepan over low heat. Stir in the lemon juice and garlic powder. Add the evaporated milk, salt, and pepper, stirring. When the mixture is hot enough that little bubbles begin to form on top around the edges, or just beginning to boil, add the dissolved cornstarch. Stir and cook for a minute or two longer, until the sauce has thickened to a chowdery-soup consistency. Remove from the heat.

Pour the sauce over the pasta and toss. Add the tuna in chunks, then toss gently. Sprinkle with parsley flakes to give color.

Serves 6

PENNE WITH TUNA, OLIVE, AND SUN-DRIED TOMATO PESTO

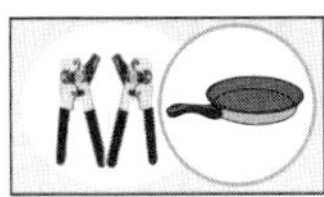

You could put just about any meat in this dish and it would taste pretty good, especially poultry. But this is another great way to use tuna, since the sun-dried tomato pesto is strong enough to hold its own against tuna's strong flavor. (An extra can of tuna works very well for those wanting extra protein.) Consider substituting green or kalamata olives, too.

One 8-ounce package penne
One 8-ounce jar sun-dried tomato pesto (or make the Sun-Dried Tomato and Walnut Pesto recipe on page 186)
One 6-ounce can tuna fish, drained and flaked
One 2.25-ounce can sliced black olives, drained
Parmesan cheese for sprinkling at the table (optional)

Make the pasta according to the package directions.

Combine the penne with the pesto and stir until well coated. Add the tuna and olives and toss. Serve immediately or reheat later.

Serve with Parmesan cheese, if desired.

Serves 4

CURRIED TUNA CAKES

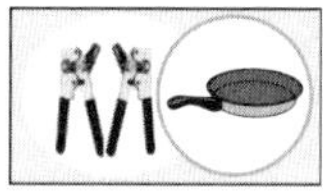

I confess I never cared much for canned tuna, but I hit upon this recipe one day while making crab puffs. It occurred to me that I could blend tuna with curry as well—a combination I hadn't tried before. The result made me a tuna eater.

These are loaded with protein and so easy to make. I keep them on hand in the fridge both for snacks and appetizers, and even for an occasional tuna melt.

10 to 12 ounces canned tuna, well drained
½ cup plain bread crumbs
2 eggs
1 teaspoon curry powder
Butter and flour for sautéing

Place the tuna into a medium-sized bowl and use two forks to pull the meat apart (think small and flaky, like crab). Add the bread crumbs. Beat two eggs (a fork is just fine for this) until they're well mixed, then add them to the tuna and crumbs. Add the curry powder and blend everything thoroughly.

Using your hands, make six cakes out of the mix (about the size of silver dollars).

Heat a skillet over medium heat, melting enough butter to sauté the tuna cakes. If you like, dredge the cakes in a little flour first, or dip them in beaten egg and more bread crumbs. Cook until they reach a rich golden-brown. Serve warm.

Serves 6

BAKED SALMON WITH WHITE WINE AND PARMESAN

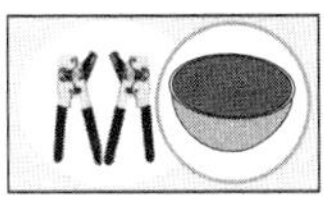

Salmon packs a lot of protein in each can. In fact, you can eat the skin and bones—they're loaded with calcium and omega acids, and they're surprisingly soft. However, I like to take out the skin and bones for aesthetic reasons. I also like to make chevrons (a herringbone pattern) on top with fork tines before baking. Consider serving this with a white sauce or a cheese sauce.

1 cup Garlic-Dill Sauce (page 182)
One 15-ounce can salmon, drained, skinned, boned, and flaked
¼ cup white wine, sherry, or beer
2 tablespoons dried chopped onion
2 teaspoons Worcestershire sauce
½ teaspoon celery salt
⅛ teaspoon cayenne pepper
1½ cups plain bread crumbs
¼ cup real grated Parmesan cheese (not powdered)
2 eggs

Preheat the oven to 350°F. Lightly oil or spray an 8×4-inch loaf pan.

Make the Garlic-Dill Sauce.

In a large mixing bowl, combine the salmon with the sauce, wine, onion, Worcestershire sauce, celery salt, and cayenne. Blend in the bread crumbs and Parmesan cheese. Lightly beat the eggs, then combine them with the salmon mixture.

Press the mixture into the pan. Bake for 35 to 40 minutes. It's ready when it gets golden-brown and slightly crisp at the edges.

Serves 8

SALMON MOUSSE MORNAY

This is a "make-ahead" dish because it requires about four hours of chilling in the refrigerator. It is quite simple, however, and requires a minimal amount of cooking—just enough to heat the liquid. Great for buffets or as a side dish. Use a lightly greased 8×4-inch loaf pan or other 6-cup mold to chill the mousse.

One 12-ounce can evaporated milk
One 10.75-ounce can cheddar cheese soup
¼ cup dry white wine, such as Chardonnay or Sauvignon Blanc
1 package unflavored gelatin
One 15-ounce can salmon, drained, bones and skin removed
½ cup sour cream
¼ cup mayonnaise
2 teaspoons onion powder
2 teaspoons Worcestershire sauce
⅛ teaspoon cayenne pepper
Dried dill (optional)

Heat the milk, cheese soup, and wine in a medium saucepan over medium-high heat, stirring to prevent burning. Heat until the mixture begins to boil (or bubbles form around the edges of the pan). Remove from the heat.

Sprinkle the gelatin over ¼ cup of cold water and let it stand about 1 minute. Stir it into the cheese-soup mixture.

In another bowl, combine the salmon, sour cream, mayonnaise, onion powder, Worcestershire sauce, and cayenne. Stir vigorously until well blended. Add to the cheese-soup mixture and blend thoroughly. Pour into the pan or mold. Chill for about 4 hours. Turn the mousse onto a plate and dust with dill before serving, if desired.

Serves 8

PASTA WITH ANCHOVY AND TOMATO

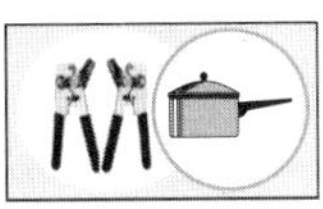

My recipe calls for less anchovies than others, so taste the sauce—you may want to add more. But if you prefer the suggestion of anchovy, as I do, just use the four. If you do, you'll have enough left from a 2-ounce tin to make a Caesar Salad (page 45). Consider serving with Baked Rosemary Loaves (page 112).

12 ounces dried penne or other pasta
3 tablespoons olive oil
1 tablespoon butter
1 teaspoon garlic powder
1 teaspoon dried parsley
½ teaspoon onion powder
4 anchovy fillets from a tin, chopped fine or mashed
One 29-ounce can crushed tomatoes
One 15-ounce can diced tomatoes, drained
½ cup grated Parmesan cheese (plus more for the table, if desired)

Cook the pasta according to the package directions.

In a medium-sized saucepan, slowly heat the oil and butter. When the butter has melted, stir in the garlic powder, parsley, and onion powder. After the spices have combined, add the anchovies and stir, cooking for about a minute. (The mixture will begin to look like a paste.) Add the tomatoes, stir, and simmer for a few minutes, until thoroughly heated.

Pour the sauce over the pasta and toss to coat. Add the Parmesan cheese and toss to coat again. Serve with additional Parmesan cheese on the side, if desired.

Serves 6

chapter 7

Breads and Pastries

CARAMEL-PECAN ROLLS

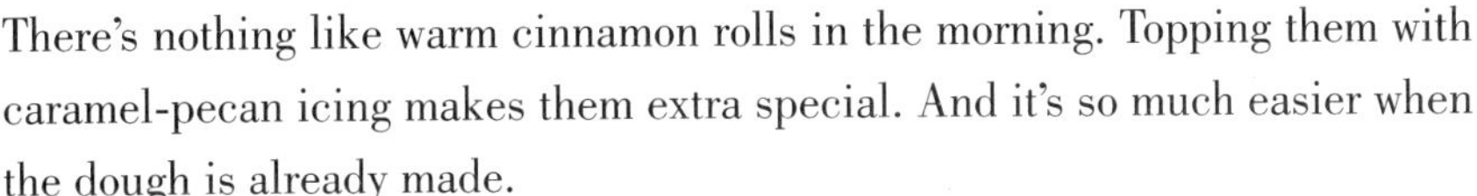

There's nothing like warm cinnamon rolls in the morning. Topping them with caramel-pecan icing makes them extra special. And it's so much easier when the dough is already made.

2 tablespoons butter
⅓ cup brown sugar
1 tablespoon light corn syrup or honey
¼ cup chopped pecans
1 can or package ready-to-bake cinnamon rolls (8 per package)

Preheat the oven to 375°F. Lightly grease or coat an 8- or 9-inch round cake pan with nonstick spray.

In a small saucepan, melt the butter, then add the brown sugar and

syrup or honey, mixing well. Bring to a boil, ensuring that everything has dissolved completely. Drizzle the syrup mixture all over the bottom of the pan (tip the pan to help coat it if needed). Sprinkle the pecans onto the syrup in the cake pan.

Unwrap the rolls, discarding the enclosed icing. Separate and place individual rolls face-down (concave side up) in the pan. In a round pan, you'll have one in the middle surrounded by the others.

Bake for 20 to 25 minutes, taking care not to overbake. When they're done, turn them out onto a plate (they come out right side up with a delicious caramel glaze).

Serves 8

RASPBERRY-PECAN CROISSANTS

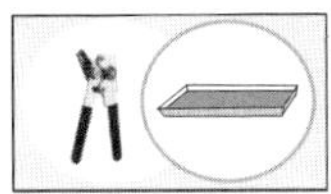

These are so easy and such a treat in the morning. I actually make them in my toaster oven. You can use just about any jam you like for these.

1 can ready-made croissant dough
Raspberry jam (about 3 tablespoons' worth)
Broken pecans (about 3 tablespoons' worth)

Preheat the oven according to the dough package instructions. If you're using a toaster oven, preheat it to 400°F. Lightly grease a baking pan that will hold eight croissants.

Separate triangles of dough. Spread a thin layer of jam on each triangle, without spreading to the edges. Sprinkle a few pecan pieces near the shortest side of the triangle (opposite the pointy end)—this is where you'll begin rolling your croissant. Roll the croissant per the package instructions.

Place the croissants on the pan and bake according to the package instructions, or until golden brown. When I baked mine in a toaster oven, they were ready in about 5 minutes.

Serves 8 to 10

MINUTE CINNAMON BISCUITS

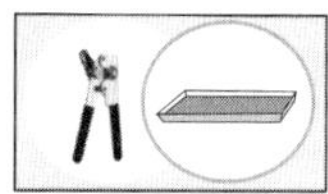

This is another morning treat. It's good even without butter.

2 tablespoons sugar
1 teaspoon cinnamon
1 can refrigerated buttermilk biscuit dough

Preheat the oven according to the dough package instructions. Lightly grease any size baking sheet. In a small bowl or dessert cup, mix the sugar and cinnamon. Dredge each biscuit in the mixture on both sides, then place on the baking sheet. Bake according to the package instructions, or until golden-brown.

BANANA PANCAKES WITH CHOPPED WALNUTS AND POWDERED SUGAR

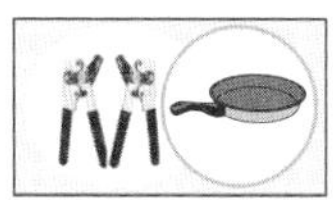

I can remember being very excited as a tyke when my dad made banana pancakes (the other dish he could make was spaghetti, also a favorite). They're such a treat for breakfast, especially when you don't have to go to the store for bananas or wait for them to ripen.

1½ cups all-purpose flour
½ teaspoon salt
2 teaspoons baking powder
¼ cup sugar
One 12-ounce can evaporated or whole milk
1 tablespoon cooking oil
1 teaspoon vanilla
Three 4-ounce jars banana baby food
1 egg, well beaten
Chopped walnuts, plain or toasted (optional)
Powdered sugar (optional)
Maple syrup (optional)

In a medium mixing bowl, whisk together the flour, salt, baking powder, and sugar so that they're thoroughly mixed. Add the milk, oil, vanilla, banana, and egg, stirring until the dry ingredients are moistened (don't overbeat). The batter will be thick—if you like a thinner batter, add a little more milk.

Heat a skillet or griddle. Spray with nonstick spray or add a little cooking oil. Drop large spoonfuls of the batter onto the hot cooking surface. When they're cooked on one side, flip the pancakes and cook on the other side. (Watch for the little bubbles to come to the surface and pop, then turn them.)

Sprinkle with chopped walnuts and powdered sugar or maple syrup, if desired.

Serves 6 (about 24 silver-dollar-sized pancakes)

OVERNIGHT FRENCH TOAST WITH TOASTED PECANS AND MAPLE SYRUP

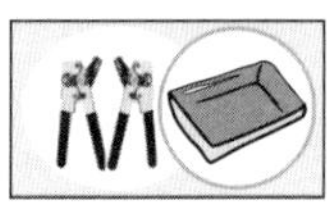

Having overnight guests? This is a special breakfast treat that you make the night before. (In fact, it can be stored for up to one day before you bake it.) It's a snap to put together.

One 24-inch baguette
4 eggs
One 12-ounce can evaporated milk or 12 ounces regular milk
1 teaspoon vanilla extract
½ teaspoon ground nutmeg
¼ teaspoon ground cinnamon
⅓ cup brown sugar, plus an additional ¼ cup for topping
½ cup chopped pecans
Real maple syrup

Lightly grease (or coat with nonstick spray) a 13×9-inch or 14×10-inch baking pan. Slice the baguette into 1-inch-thick pieces. Line the bottom of the pan with bread slices. (It's okay if they're a bit squished, and you may not need the entire loaf.)

Whisk together or beat the eggs, milk, ½ cup of water, vanilla, nutmeg, cinnamon, and ⅓ cup of the brown sugar until well blended. Pour over the bread. Sprinkle ¼ cup of brown sugar over the top, trying to distribute it evenly (it will help brown that side). Cover and chill in the refrigerator for at least eight hours and up to one day, until all of the liquid is absorbed by the bread.

When ready to bake, preheat the oven to 400°F. Put the pecans in a shallow baking pan and heat for 8 to 10 minutes to toast. Take them out and let them cool while you bake the French toast for about 25 minutes.

Top the French toast with pecans and maple syrup. Serve.

Serves 8

APRICOT BREAD WITH ALMOND AND RUM

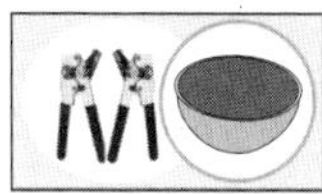

Apricot bread is perfect for afternoon tea, dessert, or a lunch-bag treat. You may make the bread with or without the almond and rum flavoring; however, I find apricot a mild fruit. For years my grandma has added almond and rum to her apricot goodies and everyone loves them. They truly enhance the fruit flavor.

One 15-ounce can apricots, drained
1¾ cups all-purpose flour
1¼ teaspoons baking powder
½ teaspoon baking soda
½ teaspoon salt
⅔ cup sugar
⅓ cup vegetable or nut oil
2 eggs
1 teaspoon almond extract (optional)
1 teaspoon rum extract (optional)

Preheat the oven to 350°F. Lightly oil or coat with nonstick spray an 8×4×2-inch baking pan.

Puree the apricots with a hand blender, blender, or food processor. (They're so soft, you could probably do it with a fork if you had to.)

In a medium-sized mixing bowl, combine the flour, baking powder, baking soda, and salt, mixing with a fork to distribute. In a larger bowl, combine the sugar and oil and beat until they're mixed. Add the eggs one at a time, beating well after each addition. Add almond and rum extracts, the apricot puree, and the flour mixture, beating until well mixed.

Pour the batter into the baking pan. Bake for 60 to 65 minutes, or until a wooden toothpick inserted into the center of the bread comes out clean. Let stand in the pan for 10 minutes to cool a bit. For easier slicing, wrap in plastic wrap and let it sit until cool.

Serves 8

BANANA-PECAN BREAD

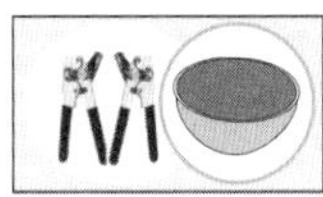

The only problem with bananas is that you have to be ready to bake banana bread when they go brown, and that doesn't always happen according to your schedule. With banana baby food you can make banana bread any time, any season. You'll also find that the texture of the bread is smoother with the pureed bananas, yet just as delicious.

1¾ cups all-purpose flour
1¼ teaspoons baking powder
½ teaspoon baking soda
½ teaspoon salt
⅔ cup sugar
⅓ cup vegetable or nut oil
2 eggs
Two 4-ounce jars banana baby food
¼ cup chopped pecans (optional)

Preheat the oven to 350°F. Lightly oil or coat with nonstick spray an 8×4-inch baking pan.

In a medium-sized mixing bowl, combine the flour, baking powder, baking soda, and salt, mixing with a fork to distribute. In a larger bowl, combine the sugar and oil and beat until they're mixed. Add the eggs one at a time, beating well after each addition. Add the baby food and the flour mixture, beating until well mixed. Stir in the pecans.

Pour the batter into the baking pan. Bake for 60 to 65 minutes, or until a wooden toothpick inserted into the center of the bread comes out clean. Let stand in the pan for 10 minutes to cool a bit. For easier slicing, wrap in plastic wrap and let it sit until cool.

Serves 8

CRANBERRY BREAD

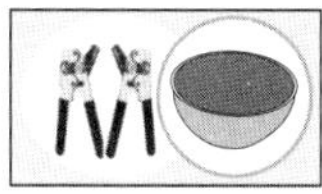

Think about making this around the winter holidays. It's a great way to use that can of cranberry sauce that's been sitting unused in your cabinet for years.

When you mash the cranberry sauce, it should be lumpy. During the baking process most of it evens out, but some of it ends up forming little pieces, which look like little chunks of fruit in the finished bread.

2 cups all-purpose flour
1/3 cup sugar
1 1/2 teaspoons baking powder
1/2 teaspoon baking soda
1/2 teaspoon salt
One 16-ounce can whole cranberry sauce, mashed with a fork
2 eggs, lightly beaten
2 tablespoons cooking oil

Preheat the oven to 350°F. Lightly oil or coat with nonstick spray an 8×4-inch loaf pan.

In a medium-sized mixing bowl, combine the flour, sugar, baking powder, baking soda, and salt, mixing with a fork to distribute. In another medium-sized mixing bowl, mash the entire can of cranberry sauce with a fork. It should be kind of lumpy when you're done. Stir in the eggs and oil. Add the flour mixture to the cranberry mixture and stir to combine. The batter should be a bit thick and stiff.

Pour the batter into the pan. Bake for 60 to 65 minutes, or until a wooden toothpick inserted into the center of the bread comes out clean. Let it stand in the pan for 10 minutes to cool. For easier slicing, wrap the bread in plastic wrap after the initial cooling period.

Serves 8

BAKED ROSEMARY LOAVES

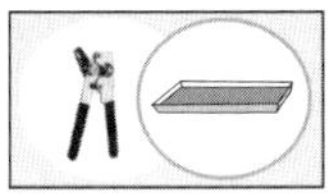

There's nothing like the smell of warm bread baking. When flavored with rosemary, these sourdough loaves make a fabulous accompaniment to many pasta, fish, and chicken dishes. They can even hold their own with beef. This recipe serves four, but it's easily doubled for more.

4 sourdough or "Italian" brown-'n'-serve rolls
2 tablespoons butter
1/4 teaspoon dried rosemary leaves, crushed or powdered

Coat a baking pan with cooking spray. Melt the butter in a small bowl in a microwave oven or in a saucepan. Split the loaves slightly, longways down the middle. Drizzle the butter across and into the loaves. Lightly dust the loaves with rosemary.

Bake the loaves according to the package instructions. Serve warm.

LEMON-GARLIC TOAST

Adding some lemon to the typical olive oil–garlic combination gives these toasts an extra dash of flavor. They're a perfect accompaniment to chicken, fish, or pasta dishes.

One 8-ounce baguette
(about 8 inches)
1 tablespoon olive oil
(or other vegetable oil in a pinch)
½ teaspoon dried parsley
½ teaspoon bottled lemon juice
⅛ teaspoon garlic powder

Set the oven to broil.

Cut the baguette on the diagonal into ½- to 1-inch slices. Broil about 4 inches from the heat source for about 2 minutes, turning once. (A toaster oven is great for this—you can watch them and turn them just as they begin to brown around the edges.)

In a small bowl or dish, combine the remaining ingredients. Drizzle (or brush) over the toasts. Serve.

Serves 4

TOASTED GARLIC PITA WEDGES

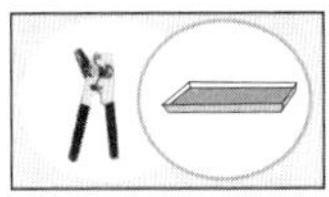

These tasty wedges are a perfect accompaniment to any Greek or Middle Eastern fare. They're also perfect for dipping into hummus, making a simple but exotic appetizer or party snack (and a healthy one, too).

1 tablespoon olive oil
1/8 teaspoon garlic powder
Three 6-inch rounds pita bread

Heat the oven to 350°F.

Pour the oil into a small bowl, sprinkle it with the garlic powder, and stir. Brush the oil lightly all over the pita round. If you don't have a brush, just drizzle a little and rub with your fingers. Slice the pita, making 6 wedges from each round.

Bake on baking sheet for about 10 minutes, or until the wedges have gotten crisp on top.

You'll have enough oil for several pita rounds. Figure about six wedges per person.

Serves 3

BLACK PEPPER CROUTONS

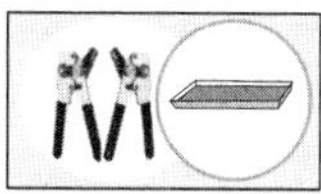

Croutons are great for soups or salads. These go quite well with Caesar Salad (page 45). Consider using a sourdough bread.

3 tablespoons olive oil
½ teaspoon garlic powder
½ teaspoon dried thyme
¼ teaspoon ground black pepper
2 cups any cubed bread, crusts removed, cut into ½-inch cubes

Preheat the oven to 325°F.

In a large frying pan, combine the oil, garlic, thyme, and pepper over medium heat. When hot, remove from the heat source. Add the bread cubes and toss to coat.

Turn the cubes out onto a baking sheet and bake for about 15 minutes, or until they just begin to turn brown. Stir a couple of times during the baking process.

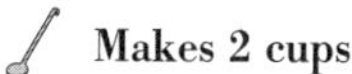

Makes 2 cups

BAKED POLENTA WEDGES WITH RED PEPPER–MANGO *COULIS*

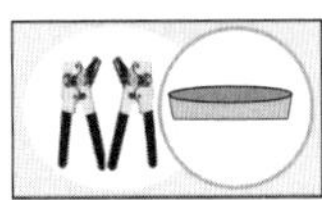

Polenta, or cornmeal, has been a staple of many cultures throughout history. It has enjoyed a sort of rediscovery more recently, serving as a creamy side dish or as a baked treat. If you haven't had baked polenta before, you should know that it won't be the consistency of cornbread—it's more like hot cereal you can pick up.

Most recipes I've seen for baked polenta use no seasoning but salt; I find that a little too bland and cheat by adding a small amount of spices. Serve with Roasted Red Pepper and Mango *Coulis* (page 202) or maybe olives, marinated artichokes, and feta cheese.

3/4 teaspoon salt
1 cup cornmeal
1/4 teaspoon sugar
1/4 teaspoon garlic powder
1/4 teaspoon onion powder
1 tablespoon olive oil or melted butter for prebake brushing

Lightly grease or coat with nonstick spray an 8- or 9-inch cake pan.

In a medium saucepan, put on 1 3/4 cups of water to boil with the 3/4 teaspoon salt. In a bowl that will hold at least 3 cups of liquid, combine the cornmeal with the sugar, garlic powder, and onion powder. Stir the dry mix with a whisk to distribute. Add 1 cup of water to the mix, stirring to combine.

When the water on the stove boils, slowly add the cornmeal mix, whisking as you do to prevent clumping. Continue cooking and whisking for several minutes (it may take anywhere from 3 to 6 minutes). When the mixture thickens enough so that a wooden spoon can stand up in it, it's ready.

Pour the mixture into the cake pan and smooth it as evenly as you can (I use a batter scraper). Let it set until cool, probably half an hour, though you can make this part up to a day ahead and then bake it when you're ready. Keep in mind that if you store it in the refrigerator, the baking time will increase.

When ready to bake, preheat the oven to 400°F. Lightly grease the baking sheet you'll use to bake the polenta. Brush a little oil or melted butter over the top of the polenta. (I haven't been able to get a good browning with olive oil.) Turn the polenta out onto a plate and brush the other side. Slice on the diagonal to produce eight triangular wedges. (If using a square pan, use perpendicular lines to make rectangular wedges.) Carefully (they'll be a little flimsy) place the wedges on your baking sheet. Bake for about 15 minutes on each side, or until the wedges begin to turn golden and a little crisp.

If you don't want to bake them, you can pan-fry them in the butter or olive oil as an alternative.

Serves 8

SAMOSAS

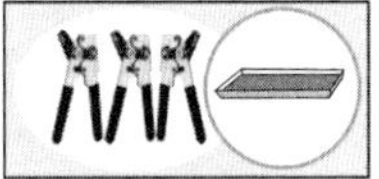

Samosas are one of my favorite Indian foods. They're usually very labor intensive, however, so I've taken a shortcut with the pastry portion of the dish. It still requires a little time and patience just to wrap the filling in the pastry, so that's why it received three can openers. But it's still quite a simple recipe.

One 14.5-ounce can sliced potatoes, drained and diced
One 8.5-ounce can sweet young peas, drained
3 tablespoons currants or chopped raisins
3 tablespoons canned diced green chili peppers
2 tablespoons bottled lemon juice
1 tablespoon soy sauce
1 tablespoon ground coriander
1 teaspoon ground cumin
1 teaspoon chili powder
¼ teaspoon ground cinnamon
3 cans ready-made refrigerated croissant dough

Preheat the oven to 400°F.

In a medium bowl, combine the potatoes, peas, currants, and chilies and gently toss. In a separate bowl, whisk the remaining ingredients, except the dough, then add to the potato mixture and toss.

Separate pastry triangles from the croissant dough. Place about 3 to 4 tablespoons of the mixture in the middle of a triangle, then cover it with another pastry triangle. Crimp the edges together with your fingers, then press the edges together firmly with fork tines. (This makes a pretty sizable samosa. For smaller pastries, such as for appetizers, use only one triangle, carefully enclosing the filling.) Place samosas on a baking sheet.

Bake for about 15 minutes, or until golden-brown. Serve with mint sauce, mango salsa, chutney, or other condiments.

Serves 12

SEASONED OYSTER CRACKERS

Fabulous on chili, clam chowder, or other soups, these crackers are so good, it's hard not to eat them right out of the bag. I sometimes use them as emergency croutons. Set them out for a Super Bowl or Oscar party snack. Though you can eat them right away, it's best if you let the flavors ripen for about 8 hours first. Oh, and they require no cooking!

2 teaspoons garlic powder
2 teaspoons onion powder
½ teaspoon salt
¼ teaspoon dried dill
¼ teaspoon paprika
¼ teaspoon dried sage
½ cup vegetable oil
½ teaspoon bottled lemon juice
One 11-ounce box oyster crackers

In a small cup, whisk the garlic powder, onion powder, salt, dill, paprika, and sage with a fork. Combine with the vegetable oil and lemon juice, whisking to blend well.

Pour the crackers into a large plastic bag. Give the oil one last whisking, then pour it over the crackers. Close the bag and shake to coat. Use your fingers on the outside of the bag to rub and distribute the oil.

On a double-thickness of paper towel, pour out the crackers and let them dry for about a half hour, during which excess oil will be absorbed by the paper. Transfer to an airtight container and let ripen for about 8 hours. Serve when ready.

Makes about 6 cups

chapter 8

Pasta and Rice

SPINACH GNOCCHI

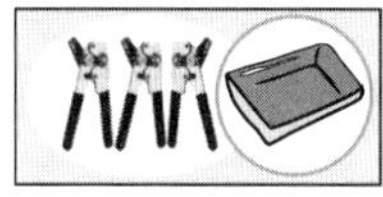

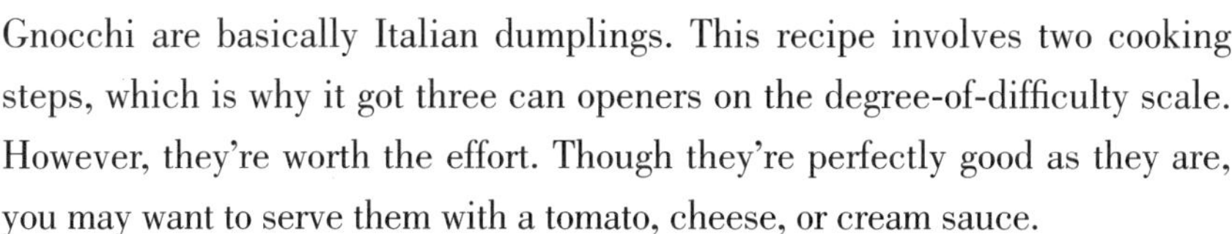

Gnocchi are basically Italian dumplings. This recipe involves two cooking steps, which is why it got three can openers on the degree-of-difficulty scale. However, they're worth the effort. Though they're perfectly good as they are, you may want to serve them with a tomato, cheese, or cream sauce.

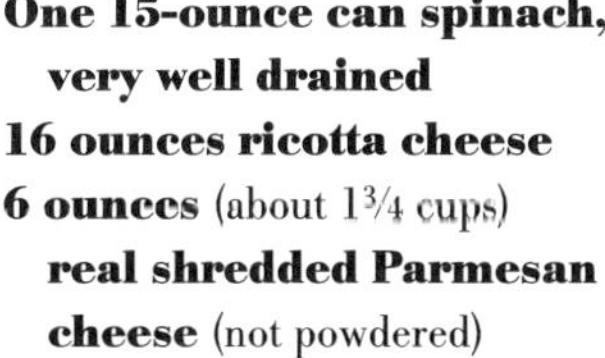

One 15-ounce can spinach, very well drained
16 ounces ricotta cheese
6 ounces (about 1 3/4 cups) **real shredded Parmesan cheese** (not powdered)
1/2 teaspoon garlic powder
3/4 teaspoon salt
1/8 teaspoon ground nutmeg
2 eggs
1 cup all-purpose flour

Drain the spinach well in a colander or sieve, pressing on it to extract as much liquid as possible. Put the spinach in a large mixing bowl and add the ricotta, half the Parmesan, garlic powder, ¼ teaspoon of the salt, and nutmeg. Stir well.

In another small bowl, beat the eggs with a fork just until they're combined and more yellow than gold. Add to the spinach mixture and stir well. Add the flour and stir until well combined.

Fill a medium saucepan about three-quarters full of water. Add the remaining ½ teaspoon of salt and place over medium-high heat to boil.

Place some waxed paper on a cutting board or another surface near the stove. To make the gnocchi, take about a tablespoonful of the spinach mix and roll it into an oblong egg shape, about 1×1½ inches. (You may want to flour your hands for this, but it's not necessary.) Place the gnocchi on waxed paper and repeat until all of the mixture has been used.

Preheat the oven to 400°F. Lightly coat a 13×9-inch baking dish or pan with vegetable oil or nonstick spray.

When the water is boiling, gently drop in about four gnocchi at a time with a slotted spoon or strainer. Cook for 2 to 3 minutes; they're ready after they float to the top. Remove them to the baking dish. Repeat until all of the gnocchi are cooked.

Sprinkle the remaining Parmesan over the gnocchi and bake for 10 minutes, until the cheese has melted.

Serve as is or with your preferred pasta sauce.

TOMATO, OLIVE, AND FETA PASTA

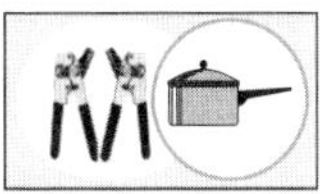

When you're low on time and low on ingredients but you still want lots of flavor, this is an easy dish that will please a variety of palates. It's also handy when you're entertaining vegetarians. Cottage cheese is a natural side dish, adding more protein to the meal. (Though one of my testers said it was terrific with ham.)

8 ounces dried pasta, such as spaghetti, linguine, or spaghettini
½ cup vegetable oil
One 15-ounce can diced tomatoes, *not* drained
One 2.25-ounce can sliced black olives, drained
1 teaspoon dried basil
1 teaspoon garlic powder
4 to 8 ounces crumbled feta cheese

Cook the pasta according to the package directions.

In a skillet or saucepan, stir together the oil, tomatoes, olives, basil, and garlic powder. Cook over medium heat, simmering gently, for about 5 minutes (can be longer if you wish). Pour over the pasta and toss. Sprinkle about ¼ cup or more of feta over the top of each serving. Great hot or cold.

Serves 4

PASTA PUTTANESCA

I like to serve this with a side of cottage cheese flavored with a little garlic powder, onion powder, or Parmesan cheese. It adds protein to this high-carb meal.

Now, about the name. I was told that pasta puttanesca was a dish once served in houses of ill repute, but I never found out if they served it to the working girls or to the customers! I've given two recipes here, one using store-bought spaghetti sauce, the other not.

12 ounces dry spaghetti

Pasta Puttanesca Sauce I

One 26-ounce jar spicy red pepper pasta sauce
One 2.25-ounce can sliced black olives, drained
1 tablespoon capers, drained

Cook the spaghetti according to the package instructions.

In a medium saucepan, mix together the pasta sauce, olives, and capers. Heat until bubbly and let simmer gently for a couple of minutes.

Toss with the pasta and serve immediately.

Pasta Puttanesca Sauce II

If you don't have spaghetti sauce or spicy spaghetti sauce on hand, you can make your own using items commonly found in your cupboard.

If you're trying to watch your salt intake, you'll like this. Did you know that tomato puree is virtually salt free? It contains only about 15 milligrams of sodium per serving.

One 29-ounce can tomato puree
One 29-ounce can diced tomatoes, drained
1 teaspoon dried basil
¾ teaspoon garlic powder
½ teaspoon cayenne pepper (or to taste)
½ teaspoon salt
½ teaspoon onion powder
One 2.25-ounce can sliced black olives, drained
1 tablespoon capers, drained

Heat all of the ingredients in a large saucepan over medium heat. Simmer for about 5 minutes. Pour over the pasta and toss.

Serves 6

WHOLE WHEAT SPAGHETTI WITH PARSLEY AND WALNUTS

Whole wheat spaghetti is now commonplace in most grocery stores. It works well combined with the nutty flavor imparted to the oil by the walnuts.

8 ounces whole wheat spaghetti
1/3 cup finely chopped walnuts
3 teaspoons dried parsley
3/4 teaspoon garlic powder
1/4 teaspoon salt
1/3 cup real fresh-grated Parmesan cheese (not powdered)
1/3 cup olive oil
Extra Parmesan cheese for sprinkling at serving time

Cook the pasta according to the package directions. Please note that whole wheat pasta may not take as long to prepare as other pastas and should not be overcooked.

Meanwhile, put the walnuts in a small bowl and add the parsley, garlic powder, salt, cheese, and oil. Stir until well blended. Pour over the cooked pasta and toss to coat.

When serving, sprinkle more Parmesan cheese over the top.

Serves 4 to 6

PENNE WITH ASPARAGUS AND LEMON CREAM SAUCE

The flavors in the lemon cream sauce here are a little stronger than those used in other cream sauces because asparagus has a stronger character. But the combination of butter and lemon with asparagus is just as compelling here in this sauce as it is simply drizzled over the vegetable, making it a good side or vegetarian dish.

12 ounces penne
4 tablespoons butter (1/2 stick)
2 tablespoons plus 1 teaspoon bottled lemon juice
1 teaspoon garlic powder
1/2 teaspoon salt
1/2 teaspoon dried parsley
One 14-ounce can chicken broth
One 12-ounce can evaporated milk
3 tablespoons cornstarch, dissolved in a little cold water
One 15-ounce can cut asparagus spears, drained
Real grated Parmesan cheese (not powdered)**, for garnish** (optional)

Make the pasta according to the package directions.

Melt the butter in a large saucepan. Stir in the lemon juice, garlic powder, salt, and parsley. Add the broth and milk. When the mixture is hot enough that little bubbles begin to form on top, or it's just beginning to boil, add the dissolved cornstarch. Stir and cook a minute or two longer, until the sauce has thickened.

Because the asparagus will break up into the sauce if too vigorously tossed, you'll want to spoon the cream sauce over the pasta first, then garnish with asparagus over the top. You may want to have additional grated Parmesan cheese at the table for sprinkling.

Serves 6

FETTUCCINE WITH PUMPKIN CREAM SAUCE

Pumpkin, like squash, is a fruit, though if you're like me you tend to think of it as a vegetable. And thinking of using it for anything but pie seemed a little odd to me. But using savory seasonings instead of sweet brings out a nice, subtle flavor from this enormous orange fruit. Turns out it makes a lovely base for a cream sauce.

You might serve this as a different and delicious side dish for fall holiday dinners. But since canned pumpkin is available year-round, consider it as a spring dish as well. The sauce becomes a rich orange color that's fitting for either season.

Consider tossing in some shelled pumpkin seeds for texture and adding a legume such as cannellini or lima beans to the grain in the pasta. And remember that pumpkin is loaded with antioxidants.

16 ounces fettuccine
One 12-ounce can evaporated milk
1 tablespoon cornstarch (Add a second tablespoon if you want a thicker sauce.)
2 tablespoons butter
One 15-ounce can pumpkin (*not* pumpkin pie filling)
1 teaspoon onion powder
1 teaspoon salt
½ teaspoon garlic powder
⅛ teaspoon dried sage
Parmesan cheese for sprinkling at the table
Shelled pumpkin seeds (optional)

Make the pasta according to the package directions. Keep warm. In a medium saucepan, whisk the milk and cornstarch together. When the cornstarch is completely dissolved, place over the stove on medium heat and add ¾ cup water, the butter, and the pumpkin. Stir. When the pumpkin is dissolved, add the onion powder, salt, garlic powder, and sage. Stir until the mixture comes to a low boil and has thickened to your liking (think alfredo sauce). If it's not thick enough for you, add 1 more tablespoon of cornstarch dissolved in a little cold water.

Toss the sauce with the fettuccine or ladle it out over the fettuccine on individual plates. Sprinkle with Parmesan cheese and pumpkin seeds, if desired.

Serves 8

FUSILLI WITH ARTICHOKE AND LEMON

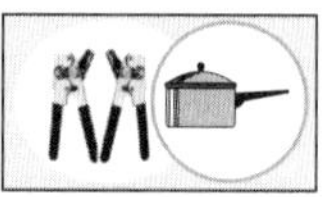

This is the vegetarian version of Fusilli with Tuna and Lemon (page 96). Fusilli is the little corkscrew pasta. If you don't have it, you can substitute just about any pasta in a pinch. If you'd like to add a legume to this grain to make a complete protein, consider adding a can of drained lima beans.

12 ounces fusilli
4 tablespoons butter (1/2 stick)
2 tablespoons bottled lemon juice
1/4 teaspoon garlic powder
One 12-ounce can evaporated milk
1/4 teaspoon salt
1/4 teaspoon ground black pepper
1 tablespoon cornstarch dissolved in a little cold water
Two 15-ounce cans chopped marinated artichoke hearts
1/2 teaspoon dried parsley

Make the pasta according to the package directions.

Melt the butter in a medium-sized saucepan over low-medium heat. Stir in the lemon juice and garlic powder. Add the evaporated milk, salt, and pepper. When it's hot enough that little bubbles begin to form on top around the edges, or it's just beginning to boil, add the dissolved cornstarch. Stir and cook for a minute or two longer, until the sauce has thickened to a chowdery-soup consistency. Remove from the heat.

Pour the sauce over the pasta. Add the artichokes, then toss. Sprinkle with the parsley flakes to give color.

Serves 6

COCONUT RICE

It's easy to add an exotic flavor to an old standby with canned coconut milk, which can be found in your grocer's Asian foods section. This rice is particularly good under curries. Don't panic if your rice isn't fluffy—it's more of a sticky rice.

Don't be afraid to make this dish if you're not a huge coconut fan. The unsweetened milk tastes like it came from fresh coconut, as opposed to the gooey-sweet taste of coconut found in many traditional confections. The result is a mild and pleasant flavoring of the rice.

One 14-ounce can unsweetened coconut milk
1/8 teaspoon salt
1 cup long-grain white rice

Combine the coconut milk, 1/2 cup of water, and salt in a saucepan and bring to a boil. Stir in the rice, reduce the heat to low, and simmer for about 15 minutes. The rice is done when the liquid has been absorbed. (Resist the urge to peek and stir, as it can make the rice stickier.) Remove the rice from the heat when done and let stand, covered, for about 5 minutes. Serve.

Serves 6

LEMON RICE

This savory rice has a nice lemony undertone. It's great with Greek dishes, Asian cuisine, and poultry.

One 14-ounce can chicken broth
1 tablespoon bottled lemon juice
½ teaspoon dried parsley
1 cup long-grain rice
1 tablespoon butter
½ teaspoon garlic powder
½ teaspoon onion powder
Salt and pepper to taste

Bring the chicken broth, ¼ cup of water, lemon juice, and parsley to a boil. Add the rice, reduce the heat, cover, and simmer for about 20 minutes (or according to the package directions). When the rice is cooked, add the butter, stirring until it has melted. Add the garlic powder and onion powder, stirring as you do to mix thoroughly. Add salt and pepper if desired.

Serves 6

CORN, TOMATO, AND PEPPER RICE

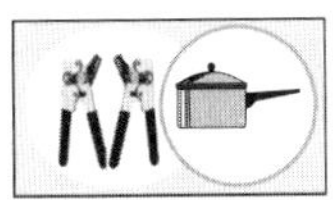

This dish is excellent served warm, but you may want to serve it chilled as a salad in the summertime as well. You can find jalapeños in your grocer's Mexican food section.

One 14-ounce can chicken broth
1 cup uncooked white rice
One 15-ounce can corn, drained
One 14.5-ounce can diced tomatoes, drained
¼ cup drained, chopped jalapeño peppers, pickled or labeled *en escabeche* (Use ½ cup if you like your rice very hot; if you like it very mild, use a 4-ounce can of plain diced chilies.)

Bring the chicken broth and ¼ cup of water to boil; add the rice. Cook according to the package directions.

If the chilies aren't chopped, chop them into small pieces (about ¼ inch long).

Add the corn, tomatoes, and chilies to the rice and stir well.

Serves 6

SPANISH RICE

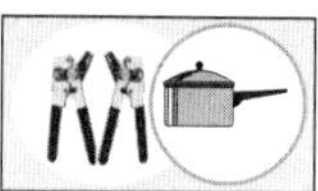

Spanish rice makes a great side dish for Mexican-themed meals and also works as a vegetarian main course. If it is to be a main course, consider adding a can of rinsed and drained pinto or black beans.

One 15-ounce can tomato sauce
One 14.5-ounce can diced tomatoes, *not* drained
One 4-ounce can diced green chilies, drained
1 tablespoon onion powder
½ teaspoon ground cumin
½ teaspoon sugar
¼ teaspoon garlic powder
¼ teaspoon dried oregano
¼ teaspoon salt
¼ cup sliced black or green Spanish olives (optional)
1 cup medium- to long-grain rice

In a large saucepan, combine all of the ingredients but the rice. Heat over medium-high heat until the mixture just begins to boil. Stir in the rice and cover. Reduce the heat and let simmer for 15 to 20 minutes, or until the rice is tender.

Serves 6

MUSHROOM RICE

Mushroom rice makes a lovely side dish for meat or poultry. I prefer brown rice for this dish because it tends not to get as sticky as white rice does. If you can find arborio rice, try that as well.

1 cup rice
One 10.5-ounce can condensed cream of mushroom soup
One 7-ounce can (net weight 4 ounces) **sliced mushrooms, drained**
1 tablespoon cream sherry (optional)

Make the rice according to the package directions.

When the rice is finished and still hot, add the mushroom soup, undiluted, and stir until absorbed (if using white rice, fluff the rice first). Add the mushrooms and sherry, if using. Serve.

Serves 6

chapter

9

Vegetables

ASPARAGUS WITH LEMON OIL AND PINE NUTS

Asparagus makes a nice change of pace as an accompaniment to many dishes. I particularly like it with quiche.

1 tablespoon pine nuts
3 tablespoons olive or vegetable oil
2 teaspoons bottled lemon juice
1/4 teaspoon garlic powder
1/4 teaspoon ground black pepper
One 15-ounce can asparagus, *not* drained

Preheat the oven to 350°F.

Toast the pine nuts on a baking sheet in the top rack of the oven for about 5 minutes, or until some turn golden-brown. (They keep cooking after you take them out.)

In a bowl, whisk the remaining ingredients except the asparagus. Heat the asparagus, then drain. Pour the oil over the asparagus and sprinkle with pine nuts.

Serves 4

WHITE ASPARAGUS WITH GARLIC-DILL SAUCE

There's something special about white asparagus. Serve chilled as (or in) a salad, or serve hot as a side dish.

1½ tablespoons cornstarch
1 cup evaporated milk
1 tablespoon butter
¼ teaspoon garlic powder
¼ teaspoon dried dill
⅛ teaspoon salt
One 15-ounce can white asparagus

Whisk the cornstarch into the milk until dissolved, then heat the milk with the butter, garlic powder, dill, and salt. Bring to a low boil, stirring until thickened.

Prepare the asparagus (heat or chill). Pour the sauce over and serve. (If chilling asparagus, chill sauce, too, and use as dressing.)

SPICY BLACK BEAN CAKES WITH SOUR CREAM AND SALSA OR TOMATO-CORN RELISH

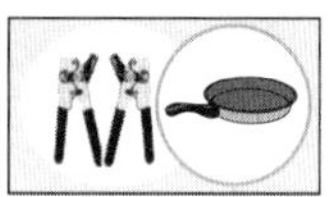

Pureeing a can of beans takes about 20 seconds with a hand blender, but you can do it manually with a potato masher. It will just require more effort. You'll find it's worth it, however, when you taste the results.

One 15-ounce can black beans, drained
1 egg
3/4 cup yellow cornmeal
1/2 teaspoon ground cumin
1/4 teaspoon salt
1/4 teaspoon ground black pepper
1/4 teaspoon onion powder
1/4 teaspoon chili powder
Flour for dredging
1 tablespoon vegetable oil
One recipe Tomato-Corn Relish (page 207) **or store-bought salsa, about 4 to 6 tablespoons**
Sour cream, about 4 to 6 tablespoons (optional)

Puree the beans. In a bowl, mix the beans with the egg. In another bowl, combine the cornmeal and all the spices, mixing with a fork to distribute, then combine with the bean mixture.

Make four to six patties from the beans. Dredge them in flour and then fry them in the oil until the outsides are browned (this takes a few minutes). Serve topped with sour cream and salsa.

Serves 4 to 6

BEANS IN BARBECUE SAUCE WITH WHISKEY

This is the same recipe for barbecue sauce found in the sauce section of the book, but I've reduced the measurements proportionally in case you just want the beans rather than a quart of sauce for barbecuing.

3/4 cup ketchup
2 tablespoons prepared mustard
1 tablespoon Worcestershire sauce
1 tablespoon maple syrup or molasses
1 tablespoon brown sugar
1/4 teaspoon garlic powder
1/4 teaspoon onion powder
1/4 teaspoon bottled lemon juice
1/8 teaspoon cayenne pepper or 1/4 teaspoon ground black pepper
1/4 teaspoon whiskey (optional)
Two 15-ounce cans ranch-style or pinto beans, drained

Combine all of the ingredients except the beans and stir. Add the drained beans and heat, in the microwave or on the stove top, to the desired temperature.

Serves 6

GREEN BEANS WITH BUTTER AND GARLIC

This recipe can be made with any style green beans—whole, French cut, or regular cut. It's amazing what a little garlic can do to a green vegetable!

2 tablespoons butter
Two 14.5-ounce cans green beans, one can drained, the other not
½ teaspoon garlic powder
¼ teaspoon salt (optional)

In a saucepan, melt the butter. Add the green beans (with the liquid of only one can) and stir to coat. Sprinkle with the garlic powder and salt (if desired). Serve when thoroughly heated.

(This dish can also easily be made in the microwave by combining everything in a large bowl and then heating on high about 2 minutes, or to the desired temperature.)

Serves 6

GREEN BEANS WITH RED PEPPER

This versatile recipe makes a nice warm side dish or a great chilled summer salad.

Two 14.5-ounce cans whole green beans, drained
2/3 cup julienne-cut roasted red peppers (from one small jar)

Vinaigrette

1/2 cup olive oil
1/4 cup rice vinegar

Put the green beans and the red peppers in a bowl (or in a saucepan if you plan to heat).

In a separate small bowl, whisk the oil and vinegar together to make a dressing. Pour the dressing over the beans and peppers and toss well. (You don't have to use all the dressing—just enough to get everything well covered.) Chill or heat to serve.

Serves 6

TRADITIONAL HOLIDAY GREEN BEANS

I just couldn't do a Can Opener Gourmet™ cookbook without including this recipe. I like to add extra seasonings to everything, and you'll see that reflected here.

One 10.75-ounce can condensed cream of mushroom soup
½ cup evaporated or whole milk
⅛ teaspoon salt
⅛ teaspoon onion powder
⅛ teaspoon garlic powder
⅛ teaspoon ground black pepper
Two 14.5-ounce cans French-style green beans, drained
One 2.8-ounce can French-fried onions

Preheat the oven to 400°F.

In an 8×8-inch baking dish, combine the soup and milk. Stir in the salt, onion powder, garlic powder, and pepper. Add the green beans and approximately half a can of the french-fried onions. Stir them together and bake, uncovered, about 10 minutes, or until they're nice and hot.

Sprinkle the remaining onions over the top of the green beans. Bake for another 5 to 10 minutes, until the onions begin to brown.

Serves 6

CARROTS GLAZED IN GINGER-LIME BUTTER

I'm not usually a cooked carrot fan, but I discovered a few years ago that when they're cooked in a tart sauce, they're pretty good. Canned carrots are surprisingly firm, too. Who knew?

2 tablespoons butter
1 tablespoon brown sugar
1 teaspoon bottled lime juice
¼ teaspoon ground ginger
One 14.5-ounce can sliced carrots, drained

Melt the butter in a medium-to-large frying pan. Add the brown sugar, lime juice, and ginger. Stir and cook for 3 to 4 minutes; add the carrots. Gently stir to coat, then let simmer for another 2 minutes or so. You want to get a nice glaze without letting the carrots begin to get soft. Serve the carrots with the lime-butter sauce poured over them.

Serves 4

HOT BUTTERED CHILI-LIME CORN

This is a great summer recipe, when served cold, as the whole dish can be made in the microwave oven, keeping the house cool. It also makes a warm spicy side dish.

2 tablespoons butter
Two 15-ounce cans corn, drained
4 teaspoons bottled lime juice
2 tablespoons drained, canned diced chili peppers (Use jalapeños if you like the dish very hot.)
Salt to taste

Combine all of the ingredients except the salt in a bowl or saucepan and heat thoroughly, until the butter has melted. In a microwave, cook 2 minutes on high. Stir to coat. Sprinkle lightly with salt and serve.

Serves 6

GLAZED BABY ONIONS

What I like about this is that you can get these onions started and then let them simmer for 15 to 20 minutes almost entirely on their own. This gives you the opportunity to "multitask" in the kitchen or chat with guests. They make a satisfyingly savory side dish for meat or poultry.

2 tablespoons butter
1 tablespoon brown sugar
Two 14.5-ounce cans white onions, well drained
1/8 teaspoon salt

In a medium-to-large frying pan, melt the butter. When melted, add sugar and stir until blended. Pour the drained onions into the pan and sprinkle with salt. Gently cook over low heat, simmering mildly, for about 15 to 20 minutes to let the liquid reduce. Stir occasionally until done.

Serves 4 to 6

MUSHROOMS SAUTÉED IN RED WINE

Mushrooms sautéed in wine make an amazingly easy side dish that lends a little elegance to your meal. Since the mushrooms are already cooked, all you need to do is coax them to accept a little butter and wine flavoring, which they willingly do. In fact, if you use red wine, they even absorb a little color, imbuing them with a slight ruby glow. Serve as a side dish or on top of red meat.

By the way, this recipe is easily doubled.

1 tablespoon butter
One 7-ounce can sliced mushrooms, drained
¼ cup red wine

Melt the butter in a saucepan. Stir in the mushrooms to coat and heat (this takes 1 to 2 minutes). Add the red wine and cook, uncovered, for a few more minutes, stirring occasionally.

Serve the mushrooms with a slotted spoon to reduce the amount of liquid on the plate.

Serves 2

VARIATION
MUSHROOMS SAUTÉED IN WHITE WINE

Follow the instructions above, but substitute ¼ cup dry white wine or sherry for the red wine.

MINTED PEAS

I suggest the "silver label" version of canned young peas that a few brands offer. They just taste fresher and firmer to me.

Two 15-ounce cans young green peas, drained
2 tablespoons butter
1 teaspoon dried mint
1 teaspoon sugar
1 teaspoon bottled lemon juice
1/4 teaspoon salt

Empty the peas into a serving bowl; set aside. Heat together the remaining ingredients and 1/4 cup of water, stirring until the butter is melted and the mint leaves are well coated and softened. Either pour the sauce directly over the peas and gently toss, or pour the peas into the saucepan and gently toss, to heat further.

Serves 6

BREAKFAST POTATOES

This recipe is easily doubled, tripled, etc. It's a terrific and quick way to make potatoes to serve with eggs. If you like, you may chop the potatoes into smaller pieces before sautéing.

1 tablespoon butter
One 15-ounce can sliced potatoes, drained
1/4 teaspoon garlic powder
1/4 teaspoon onion powder
Salt and pepper to taste

Melt the butter in a frying pan over medium heat. Stir in the potatoes and coat with butter. Sprinkle with the garlic and onion powders and sauté until thoroughly heated. It's not necessary, but if you want them to have a little brown or golden coloring, continue to cook a few minutes more.

Serves 2 generously

NEW POTATOES WITH ROSEMARY-HERB BUTTER

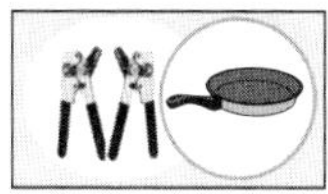

When you don't have time to clean and boil baby potatoes, this is a lifesaver—and a cooked potato is pretty much a cooked potato no matter where it hails from. This dish makes a lovely side for lamb, beef, pork, or chicken.

4 tablespoons butter (½ stick)
½ teaspoon dried, crushed rosemary leaves
¼ teaspoon garlic powder
⅛ teaspoon salt
Two 15-ounce cans whole potatoes, *not* drained

Melt the butter with the rosemary. When the butter has melted, add the garlic powder and salt.

Heat the potatoes in a microwave on high for about 2 minutes or in a small saucepan on the stove top. Drain them and then drizzle with rosemary-herb butter. Toss gently to coat. Spoon the remaining herb butter over the potatoes at serving time.

Serves 4

NEW POTATOES IN CREAM SAUCE

Baby potatoes in a rich cream sauce make a perfect side dish for beef or fish.

1 cup evaporated milk
1½ tablespoons cornstarch
1 tablespoon butter
⅛ teaspoon salt
⅛ teaspoon ground black pepper
Two 15-ounce cans whole potatoes, drained

Whisk the cornstarch into the milk until it is dissolved. Add the butter, salt, and pepper. Bring to a low boil and stir until thickened, about 3 minutes. Add potatoes and cook another 3 minutes, or until they reach the desired temperature.

Serves 4

CREAMED POTATOES AND ONIONS WITH SHERRY

This is great with beef or poultry. You may use low-fat soup and the sherry is optional.

One 10.75-ounce can condensed cream of mushroom soup
1 tablespoon sherry plus 1 tablespoon water or 2 tablespoons evaporated or whole milk
1/8 teaspoon salt
1/8 teaspoon ground black pepper
One 15-ounce can new potatoes, drained
One 15-ounce can onions, drained

Heat the soup, liquid, salt, and pepper over medium heat until smooth and hot. Add the potatoes and onions, and cook for a few minutes more, until the vegetables are thoroughly heated.

Serves 4

AU GRATIN POTATOES

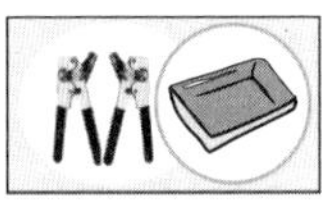

An American favorite, these potatoes are a snap to make.

One 12-ounce can evaporated milk
One 10.75-ounce can Cheddar cheese soup
1½ teaspoons onion powder
One 2.8-ounce can French-fried onions (optional)
1 tablespoon cornstarch (or 2 tablespoons flour), **dissolved in a little cold water**
Three 15-ounce cans sliced potatoes, drained

Preheat the oven to 400°F. Lightly coat a 13×9-inch baking pan with nonstick spray or vegetable oil.

In a medium saucepan, heat the milk, soup, onion powder, and onions thoroughly. When the mixture is about to boil, add the dissolved cornstarch (or flour). Cook and stir for a couple of minutes more while the mixture thickens. Remove from the heat.

Empty the potatoes into the baking pan, separating and spreading them. Pour the hot cheese mix over the potatoes, then bake for 35 to 40 minutes, or until the edges begin to turn golden-brown.

Serves 6 to 8

SOUR CREAM–BAKED POTATOES AND BACON

This recipe came to me from my grandma, Laura E. Karr. She uses a package of ranch dressing mix to season the sour cream. Here, I've used spices so that you're not dependent on having the packaged mix around.

You may use low-fat or nonfat sour cream, which tends to be thinner and more easily stirred. If you use regular sour cream, you may want to add 2 tablespoons of evaporated or whole milk, or 2 tablespoons of liquid from the potatoes to thin it out. Use as much as needed to give it a consistency that will coat the potatoes.

1 pint (2 cups) **sour cream**
1 teaspoon onion powder
1 teaspoon garlic powder
½ teaspoon dried parsley
½ teaspoon salt
¼ cup real grated Parmesan cheese (not powdered)
¼ cup bottled real bacon pieces
Three 15-ounce cans sliced potatoes, drained

Preheat the oven to 300°F. Lightly grease or coat with nonstick spray a 13×9-inch pan or dish.

In a medium-sized mixing bowl, combine all ingredients except the potatoes, stirring well. If needed, add milk or potato liquid to thin. Add the drained potatoes and toss to coat.

Empty the potato mixture into the baking dish and cook for about 30 minutes, or until thoroughly heated.

Serves 6 to 8

chapter 10

Eggs and Cheese

BREAKFAST BAKE

This dish is convenient because you can let it sit overnight, covered, in your refrigerator and then just pop it in the oven in the morning (this will require extra cooking time, however). You can bake it right away, too. It's great for when you want an easy but impressive next-morning brunch food.

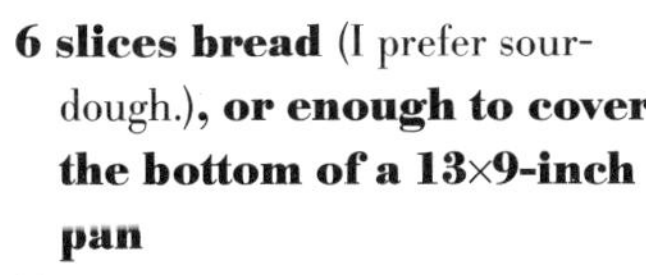

6 slices bread (I prefer sourdough.)**, or enough to cover the bottom of a 13×9-inch pan**
6 eggs
One 12-ounce can evaporated milk
½ teaspoon salt
¼ teaspoon onion powder
¼ teaspoon ground black pepper
¼ teaspoon garlic powder
1½ cups shredded Cheddar cheese
One 5-ounce can ham, drained and diced

Preheat the oven to 350°F. Grease or coat a 13×9-inch baking pan with nonstick spray. Line the entire bottom of the pan with bread slices (you may remove the crusts first if you wish).

In a bowl, whisk together the eggs, milk, and spices. Add the cheese and stir again. Pour over the bread. Sprinkle diced ham bits evenly across the top. Bake for 30 to 35 minutes, or until the eggs are set.

Serves 8

SCRAMBLED EGGS WITH FETA CHEESE AND OLIVES

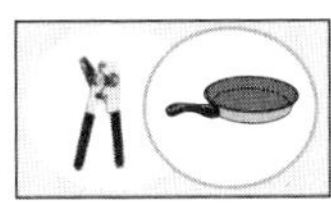

Here's an easy way to dress up scrambled eggs in a hurry. Serve with some seasoned potatoes and you have a flavorful breakfast. You'll need about 1 tablespoon of olives and 2 tablespoons of feta cheese for every 2 eggs.

8 eggs
One 2.25-ounce can black sliced olives, drained
One 4-ounce container crumbled feta cheese

Lightly oil or spray a frying pan, then place it over medium heat. Crack the eggs into the pan, then add the olives and cheese. Stir with a spatula until the eggs have cooked but are not dry. Serve warm.

HUEVOS RANCHEROS

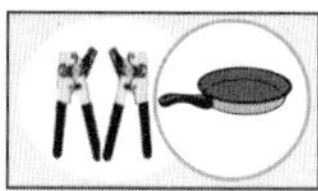

Some folks like their eggs sunny-side-up for this dish, while others like them scrambled. Because it's easier, especially if you're feeding more than two people, I've used the scrambled method. (And just so you know, you can freeze the tortillas for storage before use!)

6 corn tortillas
Cooking oil for tortillas
16 ounces (more if you like) **good chunky salsa**
One 15-ounce can black beans, rinsed and drained (optional)
6 to 12 eggs (Allow 1 or 2 eggs per person.)
Salt to taste
1½ cups shredded Cheddar or Jack cheese (more if you like a lot of cheese)
Pinch dried cilantro

Lightly coat a baking sheet with oil or nonstick spray.

Lightly fry the tortillas one at a time in a little oil. As an alternative, you may brush the tortillas with oil and bake them at 400°F until they begin to brown, about 10 minutes. Drain on paper towels if needed and keep warm.

If you haven't done so in order to cook the tortillas, preheat the oven to 400°F.

Place the cooked tortillas on the prepared baking sheet. Heat the salsa a little if it has been in the refrigerator. Otherwise, spread each tortilla with enough salsa to cover it (about ¼ cup). Add beans if desired.

Make scrambled eggs, then divide them atop the salsa-covered tortillas. Lightly salt the eggs, then sprinkle each with about 3 tablespoons of cheese (more if you like). Lightly dust with a little dried cilantro.

Bake until the cheese melts—check after 2 minutes. When the cheese has melted, serve at once.

Serves 6

QUICK SHRIMP QUICHE

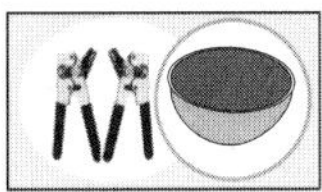

Seafood quiche is a lovely brunch dish because it's elegant yet easy. After mixing everything together, you can slip it into the oven and slip out of the kitchen for a while. As a brunch dish, it's nice with Breakfast Potatoes (page 150). If you're serving it at dinner, try it with Asparagus with Lemon Oil and Pine Nuts (page 137) or Creamy Green Beans and Potatoes (page 38).

3 eggs
⅓ cup evaporated or whole milk
2 teaspoons onion powder
½ teaspoon Worcestershire sauce
¼ teaspoon bottled lemon juice
Pinch ground nutmeg
One 4.25-ounce can tiny shrimp, drained
1 cup shredded Swiss cheese
1 frozen 9-inch pie crust

Preheat the oven to 425°F.

In a medium-sized mixing bowl, whisk together the eggs, milk, onion powder, Worcestershire sauce, lemon juice, and nutmeg. Gently stir in the shrimp and cheese. Pour into the frozen piecrust. Bake for 35 minutes, or until a knife inserted into the middle comes out clean.

Serves 6

VARIATIONS

QUICK CRAB QUICHE

Follow the instructions above, but substitute one 4.25-ounce can of crab, drained and flaked, cartilage removed, for the shrimp.

QUICK SMOKED SALMON QUICHE

Follow the instructions above, but substitute one 6.5-ounce can smoked salmon, drained and flaked, for the shrimp.

MUSHROOM-BACON QUICHE

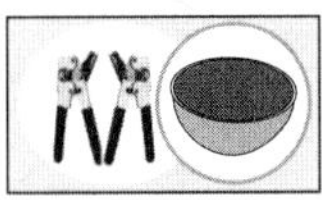

Sure, I'm prone to a little exaggeration, but this is probably the easiest quiche there is. It's great served with creamed potatoes and either asparagus or green beans.

3 eggs
⅓ cup evaporated or whole milk
1 cup shredded Cheddar cheese
One 7-ounce can (net weight 4 ounces) **sliced mushrooms, drained**
1 ounce real bacon pieces (half of a 2-ounce bottle)
Half of a 4-ounce can sliced black olives, drained (optional)
1 frozen 9-inch pie crust

Preheat the oven to 425°F.

In a medium-sized mixing bowl, combine the eggs, milk, cheese, mushrooms, bacon, and olives. Pour into the frozen piecrust. Bake for 35 minutes, or until a knife inserted into the middle comes out clean.

Serves 6

EGGS STUFFED WITH LEMON AND TARRAGON

In my opinion, tarragon can easily become overpowering, so I've used it sparingly in this dish. If you're a big tarragon lover, you may want to add more. This makes a great high-protein snack or party appetizer.

6 eggs
1 teaspoon bottled lemon juice
½ teaspoon dried tarragon
¼ cup mayonnaise
½ teaspoon prepared Dijon mustard
¼ teaspoon garlic powder
¼ teaspoon onion powder

Place the eggs in a medium-sized saucepan and cover with water. Bring to a rapid boil, then turn down to a low boil and cook for 10 to 12 minutes. Remove from the heat and fill the pan with cold water to stop the eggs from cooking. After the eggs have cooled, peel them.

In a small cup, combine the lemon juice and tarragon. Let stand for a couple of minutes so that some liquid is absorbed.

Meanwhile, slice the eggs vertically and remove the yolks. In a bowl, combine the yolks with the remaining ingredients, including the lemon juice and tarragon. Stir and mash well with a fork.

Place scoops of the yolk mixture back into the hollows of the eggs and serve.

Makes 12 stuffed egg halves

EASY CHEESE FONDUE

Cheese fondue is such a fun thing to serve at a dinner party. I make it each year during the holidays, but it's appreciated at any time.

Two 10-ounce cans Cheddar cheese soup
One 12-ounce can evaporated milk
1 teaspoon Worcestershire sauce
½ teaspoon dry mustard
⅛ teaspoon salt
⅔ cup beer or ½ cup dry white wine
1 tablespoon cornstarch dissolved in a little cold water
Cut-up vegetables, sourdough bread cut into cubes, or other dipping foods

Combine the soup, milk, Worcestershire sauce, mustard, salt, and beer or wine in a saucepan. Cook over medium heat, stirring constantly, until the lumps are gone and the cheese is smooth and creamy (it should reach a soft boil). Add the cornstarch dissolved in water and stir until the cheese has thickened to proper fondue consistency (much like a thick chowder).

Pour into a fondue pot and serve with dipping treats.

Makes just over 3 cups

CREAM CHEESE AND OLIVE SPREAD

If you want to dress up a bagel or wheat crackers or make a special sandwich, this is a quick and easy way to do it. Consider using green stuffed Spanish olives (though you'll have to chop them yourself).

If you want to hurry the "room temperature" part a bit, put the unwrapped cream cheese in the microwave and zap it on high for 15 seconds. Otherwise, just let it sit for about an hour, or until it's easier to mix.

One 8-ounce package cream cheese, at room temperature
One 4-ounce can chopped black olives, drained

In a small mixing bowl, combine the cream cheese and olives, stirring until well mixed.

Makes about 8 one-ounce servings (one ounce covers an entire bagel)

CRUSTLESS CHEESE TART

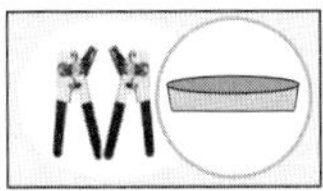

This simple tart makes a good breakfast food (try sprinkling some bottled real bacon pieces on top) or a savory side dish.

One 12-ounce can evaporated milk
1 cup shredded Cheddar cheese
¼ teaspoon onion powder
¼ teaspoon salt
Pinch cayenne pepper
3 eggs

Preheat the oven to 325°F. Lightly grease or coat with nonstick spray an 8- to 9-inch cake or tart pan.

Heat the milk and ¼ cup of water in a saucepan over medium-high heat, stirring occasionally so nothing burns on the bottom. When it just begins to boil, reduce the heat and add the cheese, stirring until completely dissolved. Add the onion powder, salt, and cayenne. Remove from the heat.

In a small bowl, beat the eggs until they're well combined and lemon-colored. Stir a little bit of hot cheese mixture into the eggs to warm them, then slowly pour the eggs into the cheese mixture, stirring well.

Pour the mixture into the prepared pan. Bake for about 40 minutes, or until a knife stuck in the middle comes out clean

Serves 6

CORN PUDDING WITH DICED CHILIES

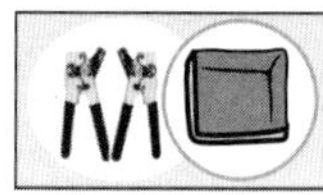

Corn pudding makes a great side dish for Southwestern or Mexican fare. Cooking it in the microwave eliminates the need to put the pan in hot water in the oven. However, for those who don't wish to use the microwave, I've included directions for oven baking below.

3 eggs
One 12-ounce can evaporated milk
One 15-ounce can whole-kernel corn, drained
2 teaspoons onion powder
1 teaspoon sugar
One 4-ounce can diced chili peppers, drained

Lightly grease or coat with nonstick spray an 8-inch pan or pie dish.

In a medium-sized mixing bowl, beat the eggs until they are more lemon-colored than gold. Add the milk and beat or whisk until blended. Stir in the remaining ingredients, then pour into the prepared dish.

Microwave on high for 10 minutes, or until a knife inserted in the center comes out clean.

For oven cooking:

Preheat the oven to 350°F. Lightly grease or coat with nonstick spray 8-inch cake pan.

Pour the mixed ingredients into the pan. Place the pan in a larger pan, then fill the larger pan with hot water up to 1 inch in depth. Bake for 25 to 30 minutes, or until a knife inserted in the center comes out clean.

Serves 6

SUN-DRIED TOMATO AND CHEESE ENCHILADAS

Making food with authentic flavor doesn't have to be hard. You may use prepared enchilada sauce (which you can find in your grocer's ethnic foods section), or make your own with the recipe provided below. If you're not a sun-dried tomato fan, you can substitute prepared salsa or canned diced tomatoes, or simply use the enchilada sauce.

Homemade Enchilda Sauce

One 15-ounce can tomato sauce
1 teaspoon garlic powder
1 teaspoon onion powder
¾ teaspoon dried oregano
½ teaspoon ground cumin
½ teaspoon dried cilantro
¼ teaspoon sugar
⅛ to ¼ teaspoon cayenne pepper

One 19-ounce can enchilada sauce or Homemade Enchilada Sauce
1 cup grated Cheddar or Jack cheese
4 small tortillas
2 tablespoons sun-dried tomatoes (optional)
One 2.25-ounce can sliced black olives
16 ounces prepared salsa or one 15-ounce can diced tomatoes, drained, or one 4-ounce can diced chilies, drained (all optional)

In a large bowl, combine all of the sauce ingredients.

For microwave cooking:

Sprinkle about ¼ cup shredded cheese and a couple of tablespoonsful of sauce on an open tortilla. Place a few sun-dried tomatoes, diced tomatoes, or some salsa on top, along with the olives and/or chilies. Heat, unfolded, in a microwave oven until the cheese melts. Fold like a burrito (fold ⅓ tortilla over, bottom ⅓ up, then roll). Garnish with additional sauce, cheese, and olives, if desired.

For oven cooking:

Preheat the oven to 400°F. The baking sheet or dish (any size) needs no preparation.

Briefly heat the tortillas so that they're workable. Fill the tortillas as described above. Fold like a burrito as described above. Place on the baking sheet or in the dish and continue with the other enchiladas. Cover with the remaining sauce, and sprinkle with a little extra cheese and olives if desired.

Bake for about 10 minutes, or until the cheese inside melts.

Serves 4

GREEK FETA AND SPINACH PASTRIES

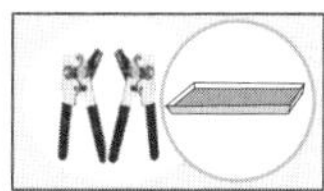

I adapted this recipe from one for the Greek pastry *spanakopitta,* which requires extensive work with phyllo dough. If you haven't worked with phyllo before, hear me when I say that it's not for those with a low frustration tolerance (like myself). I used similar ingredients here but substituted a ready-to-bake pastry dough for the finicky phyllo. These pastries are great either as an appetizer or a side dish.

One 15-ounce can spinach, drained
2 teaspoons bottled lemon juice
8 ounces crumbled feta cheese
3 eggs
4 cans refrigerated crescent roll dough

Preheat the oven to 400°F. Lightly grease or coat a cookie sheet with nonstick spray.

Drain the spinach in a large strainer or colander as best you can, pressing it against the sides and squeezing out excess moisture. In a medium-sized bowl, mix the drained spinach, lemon juice, and feta. In another small bowl, beat the eggs until very well mixed—they should be less gold-colored and more of a soft lemon color. Add them to the spinach mixture and stir thoroughly.

Open the crescent dough can and pull the dough triangles apart.

Spoon about a heaping tablespoon of spinach mixture onto one triangle, spreading it as evenly as you can without letting it run off the sides. Cover with another triangle and pinch all of the sides together, sealing the spinach in the pastry. You will have what looks like a popover. Continue with the remaining cheese mixture and pastries.

Place the pastries on the baking sheet and bake for about 15 minutes, or until they're plumped and golden-brown.

Makes about 16 pastries

PESTO PIZZA WITH CORN AND ROASTED RED PEPPERS

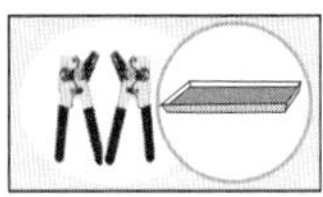

Pizza is one of those foods that allows for a nearly infinite number of variations. This is one of my favorites and was actually one of the first dishes that got me thinking about using canned foods. (What, I was going to boil corn cobs and then scrape off the kernels for the pizza?) You can easily double the recipe, as it calls for only half the corn and peppers. A 10-ounce jar of pesto makes two pizzas.

1 large premade pizza crust (see Note)
1 small jar pesto sauce (at least 6 ounces)
2½ cups shredded mozzarella or Jack cheese
One 15-ounce can corn, drained
½ cup julienne-cut roasted red peppers from a jar
(If you can't find them precut, just cut them into small or thin pieces.)

Preheat the oven to 450°F or as the packaged pizza crust directions indicate. Prepare the pizza tin or cookie sheet with nonstick spray if desired.

Spread a layer of pesto sauce over the pizza crust—you will need about 1 cup. Cover with the shredded cheese. Sprinkle about ½ cup corn (more if you like) over the cheese. Place several pieces of roasted red peppers on top of that. Bake for about 12 minutes, or until the cheese is melted and bubbly.

 Serves 8

Note: If you use a frozen crust, be sure to check the directions in case you need to prebake it or thaw it.

HAM AND PINEAPPLE PIZZA

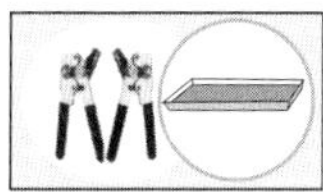

This pizza would work well for a Hawaiian-themed event, or any time you need a quick pizza. Lots of folks love the sweet-and-salty combination provided by the fruit and ham.

1 large ready-made pizza crust (see Notes)
1 cup pizza sauce (see Notes)
2½ cups shredded mozzarella or Jack cheese
One 5-ounce can ham, drained and diced (you may wish to use only half the can, depending on how much you like)
One 8-ounce can pineapple chunks, drained (you may want to save the pineapple juice and mix it with coconut milk for a tropical beverage)

Preheat the oven to 450°F or as the packaged pizza crust directions indicate. Prepare pizza tin or cookie sheet with nonstick spray if desired.

Spread a layer of pizza sauce onto the crust. Cover that with shredded cheese. Sprinkle with diced ham and pineapple chunks. Bake for 10 to 12 minutes, or until the cheese is melted and bubbly.

Notes: If you use a frozen crust, be sure to check the directions in case you need to prebake it or thaw it.

Use ready-made spaghetti or pizza sauce, or use my easy Homemade Pizza Sauce recipe (see page 187).

SPANISH OLIVE, BACON, AND SUN-DRIED TOMATO PESTO PIZZA

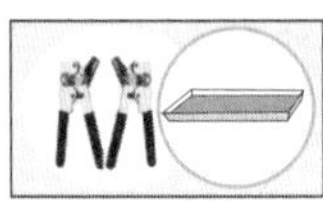

This is for the die-hard pizza lover looking for a lot of flavor. The sun-dried tomato pesto gives it some extra zing and makes a nice backdrop for the olives and bacon.

1 large ready-made pizza crust (see Notes)
1 cup sun-dried tomato pesto (see Notes)
2½ cups shredded mozzarella or Jack cheese
½ cup chopped stuffed Spanish olives
¼ cup bottled real bacon pieces

Preheat the oven to 450°F or as the packaged pizza crust directions indicate. Prepare pizza tin or cookie sheet with nonstick spray if desired.

Spread a thin layer of pesto onto the crust. Cover with the shredded cheese. Sprinkle with olives and bacon pieces. Bake for 10 to 12 minutes, or until the cheese is melted and bubbly.

Serves 8

Notes: If you use a frozen crust, be sure to check the directions in case you need to prebake or thaw it.

Use ready-made pesto, or use my easy recipe (see page 186). You may also use my Homemade Pizza Sauce recipe (see page 187).

chapter 11

Sauces and Dressings

BASIC WHITE SAUCE

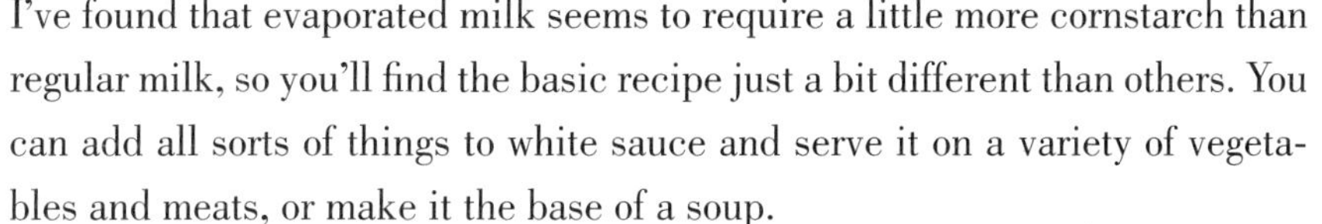

I've found that evaporated milk seems to require a little more cornstarch than regular milk, so you'll find the basic recipe just a bit different than others. You can add all sorts of things to white sauce and serve it on a variety of vegetables and meats, or make it the base of a soup.

1½ tablespoons cornstarch
1 cup evaporated milk
1 tablespoon butter
⅛ teaspoon salt

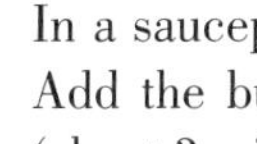

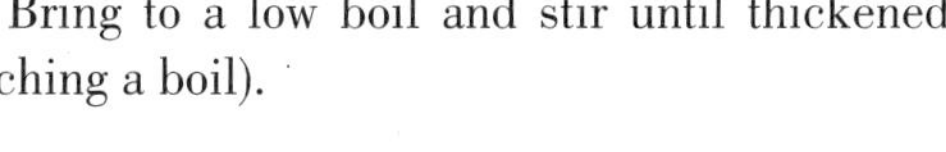

In a saucepan, whisk the cornstarch into the cold milk until dissolved. Add the butter and salt. Bring to a low boil and stir until thickened (about 3 minutes after reaching a boil).

Makes about 1 cup

Note: To double this recipe, use one 12-ounce can of evaporated milk plus ½ cup water, then double the remaining ingredients.

LEMON CREAM SAUCE

Lemon cream sauce is so good on so many things—pasta, rice, asparagus, broccoli, even as a substitute for hollandaise sauce on egg dishes. The advantage here is no eggs.

4 tablespoons butter (1/2 stick)
One 14-ounce can chicken broth
One 12-ounce can evaporated milk
2 tablespoons bottled lemon juice
1/2 teaspoon dried parsley
1/4 teaspoon garlic powder
3 tablespoons cornstarch dissolved in a little cold water
Salt and pepper to taste (Try 1/8 teaspoon each.)

Melt the butter in a saucepan over medium heat. Stir in the broth, milk, lemon juice, parsley, and garlic powder. When the mixture is hot enough that little bubbles begin to form on top around the edges, or it's just beginning to boil, add the dissolved cornstarch. Stir and cook for a few minutes longer, until the sauce has thickened. Add salt and pepper.

Makes about 3 cups

TART LEMON CREAM SAUCE

Use this sauce for strong-flavored meats such as tuna, ham, smoked salmon, or sardines.

4 tablespoons butter (1/2 stick)
1/4 cup bottled lemon juice
1/4 teaspoon garlic powder
One 14-ounce can chicken broth
One 12-ounce can evaporated milk
1/2 teaspoon dried parsley
1/4 teaspoon salt
1/4 teaspoon ground black pepper
3 tablespoons cornstarch dissolved in a little cold water

Melt the butter in a medium-sized saucepan over low-medium heat. Stir in the lemon juice and garlic powder. Add the chicken broth, evaporated milk, parsley, salt, and pepper, stirring. When the mixture is just beginning to boil, add the dissolved cornstarch. Stir and cook a couple of minutes longer, until the sauce has thickened to a chowdery-soup consistency. Remove from the heat.

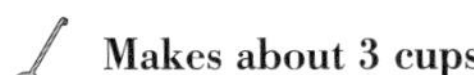

Makes about 3 cups

CHEESE SAUCE

This is a basic cheese sauce that tastes terrific on vegetables, rice, and noodles. Try it on salmon, too.

One 12-ounce can evaporated milk, or 1½ cups whole milk
2 tablespoons cornstarch
1 tablespoon butter
¼ teaspoon salt
1 cup shredded Cheddar or Swiss cheese

In a small saucepan, whisk together the milk and cornstarch until the cornstarch is dissolved. Add the butter and salt and cook over medium-high heat, stirring to keep the bottom from sticking. When the butter is melted, add the cheese and cook, stirring, until the cheese is completely melted and the sauce has thickened (about 2 to 3 minutes after the cheese has melted).

VARIATION

SHERRIED CHEESE SAUCE

Follow the instructions above, but add 1 tablespoon of sherry as sauce begins to thicken.

CURRY SAUCE

Don't be frightened by the number of spices in this sauce—it's very, very simple. Indian cuisine, however, tends to consist of a series of complex, seemingly opposite flavors thrown together and somehow becoming a harmonious, intoxicating blend. It borders on miraculous if you ask me.

You may also be surprised to see Worcestershire sauce as an ingredient here. The reason? Most American cooks do not keep tamarind seeds as a spice, yet tamarind is an essential ingredient in many Indian curries. Tamarind, however, is an ingredient in some Worcestershire sauces. And it turns out Worcestershire sauce has many of the ingredients one finds in a curry, so it works.

Curries are fabulous with just about any meat, but they're especially popular with chicken, lamb, beef, and shrimp. This one's also extremely low in fat.

One 29-ounce can tomato sauce
1 tablespoon olive oil
1 tablespoon plus 1 teaspoon Worcestershire sauce with tamarind (So far I've seen it only in Lea & Perrins' brand.)
1½ tablespoons onion powder
2 teaspoons curry powder
1½ teaspoons sugar
½ teaspoon chili powder
½ teaspoon ground ginger
¼ teaspoon garlic powder
¼ teaspoon ground cinnamon
⅛ teaspoon cayenne pepper (more if you like your sauce hotter)

Combine all of the ingredients in a medium-sized nonaluminum saucepan and bring to a low boil. Simmer gently for at least a few minutes so that the flavors can blend (longer is fine, too). It's ready to serve when you are.

Makes about 2½ cups, enough for 5 to 6 servings

OLIVE-RAISIN-WINE SAUCE

Great for chicken, lamb, or pork! The recipe makes enough for about four chicken breasts. Serve them with spiced black beans and rice for a Cuban flair.

1 cup canned chicken broth, or ½ cup chicken bouillon plus ½ cup water
½ cup dry red wine, or ⅓ cup broth plus 2 tablespoons balsamic vinegar
2 tablespoons olive oil
One 4.25-ounce can chopped black olives, drained
½ cup currants or chopped raisins
½ teaspoon garlic powder
½ teaspoon dried marjoram
¼ teaspoon onion powder
1 tablespoon cornstarch dissolved in a little cold water

In a saucepan, combine all of the ingredients except the cornstarch. Bring to a boil, then reduce the heat and simmer for about 5 minutes.

Add the dissolved cornstarch to the hot broth mixture. Cook for another 2 minutes or so, stirring until it has thickened.

Makes about 2 cups

GARLIC-DILL SAUCE

I think garlic and dill were made for each other. And while this sauce is packed with flavor, it's not overpowering.

1½ tablespoons cornstarch
1 cup evaporated milk
1 tablespoon butter
¼ teaspoon garlic powder
¼ teaspoon dried dill
⅛ teaspoon salt

Whisk the cornstarch into the milk until it has dissolved, then heat the milk with the remaining ingredients. Stir and bring to a low boil until thickened.

Makes about 1 cup

Note: To double this recipe, use one 12-ounce can of evaporated milk plus ½ cup water, then double the remaining ingredients.

SWEET ORANGE-BASIL SAUCE

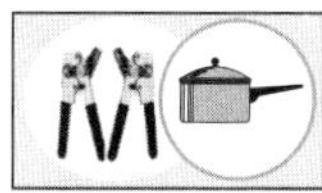

I've used this recipe in a shrimp dish, but it would be suitable for chicken, turkey, duck, or pork as well. It's very low in fat, too.

1 teaspoon or cube chicken bouillon
One 8-ounce box, bottle, or can orange juice
1 tablespoon sherry
1 teaspoon sugar
½ teaspoon dried basil
3 tablespoons cornstarch dissolved in a little cold water

In a medium saucepan, heat 1¾ cups water and the bouillon cube until the bouillon dissolves. Or just add the teaspoon of bouillon when heating the water. Add the orange juice, sherry, sugar, and basil. Bring to a boil, then add the dissolved cornstarch and stir over medium heat until thickened.

Makes about 3 cups

BARBECUE SAUCE WITH WHISKEY

The tangy, sweet-and-spicy tastes of a summer barbecue are served right up in this delicious sauce. It makes well over 3 cups—enough to barbecue about twelve pieces of chicken or ribs and to save 3/4 cup or so to make Beans in Barbecue Sauce with Whiskey (page 141).

3 cups ketchup
1/2 cup prepared mustard
1/4 cup Worcestershire sauce
1/4 cup maple syrup or molasses
1/4 cup brown sugar
1 tablespoon whiskey (optional)
1 teaspoon garlic powder
1 teaspoon onion powder
1 teaspoon bottled lemon juice
1/4 to 1/2 teaspoon cayenne pepper

Combine all of the ingredients and stir. Baste meats during the last 5 minutes of barbecuing.

Makes a little over 4 cups

GREEK GARLIC LEMON MARINADE

This highly flavored oil is something you can easily brush on chicken or lamb for barbecuing, baking, or sautéing—dishes that are especially good served with lemon rice and hummus.

¼ cup olive oil
2 teaspoons bottled lemon juice
1 teaspoon garlic powder

Combine the ingredients and whisk together. The garlic will tend to fall to the bottom, but it will be picked up with your brush or baster.

To barbecue or bake, brush on liberally before cooking, reapplying during the cooking process. To sauté, pour the flavored oil into the frying pan and cook as you would normally.

Coats 4 to 6 pieces of meat or poultry

SUN-DRIED TOMATO AND WALNUT PESTO

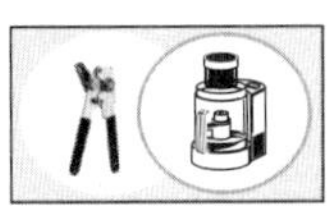

Sun-dried tomato pesto is so versatile, as well as being a tasty way to get some of the benefits of olive oil and vitamin A. This recipe makes about 2 cups—enough for both a pasta dinner for 6 and a recipe of Parmesan, Pesto, and Sun-Dried Tomato Toasts (page 25). It also makes a savory pizza sauce or cracker spread.

1/4 cup finely chopped walnuts
One 8-ounce jar julienne-chopped sun-dried tomatoes packed in oil, drained (If you're using another size jar, you'll need about 1 1/2 cups drained sun-dried tomatoes.)
3/4 cup olive oil
1 teaspoon garlic powder
1/4 teaspoon salt
3/4 cup real grated Parmesan cheese (not powdered)

Toast the walnuts. You may put them in a baking pan on the top rack of your oven set at 350°F and bake for about 10 minutes, put them in a toaster oven on medium toast, or heat them over the stove in a nonstick pan until they begin to crackle.

Drain the sun-dried tomatoes. With a food processor or hand blender, process the tomatoes, walnuts, olive oil, garlic powder, salt, and Parmesan cheese until you have a pastelike sauce and everything is blended together.

You may serve it immediately or store it up to a week in an airtight container in the refrigerator. It may also be served warm. Simply heat on medium-high in a microwave for a few minutes.

Makes about 2 cups

HOMEMADE PIZZA SAUCE

Pizza sauce in an instant! This can easily be doubled if you're making two pizzas.

One 8-ounce can tomato sauce
½ teaspoon sugar
½ teaspoon dried basil
¼ teaspoon garlic powder
¼ teaspoon onion powder

Combine all of the ingredients in a small bowl and stir.

Makes about 1 cup (enough for one pizza)

SPAGHETTI SAUCE

Whether you're caught without a jar of spaghetti sauce or just interested in making a more interesting, low-sodium variation, this is a great-tasting red sauce that's quick to make. It's generally lower in sodium than store-bought sauce, as tomato puree has only about 15 milligrams of sodium per serving.

Two 28-ounce cans tomato puree
One 28-ounce can diced tomatoes, *not* drained
1 teaspoon garlic powder
½ teaspoon onion powder
½ teaspoon salt
½ teaspoon sugar
1 teaspoon dried basil
Two 7-ounce cans sliced mushrooms, drained (optional)
1 pound cooked ground beef (optional)

In a large saucepan, combine all of the ingredients. Bring to a boil, then lower the heat and simmer, stirring, for about 5 minutes (or longer if you wish).

Makes at least 7 cups; more if you add meat

PUTTANESCA SAUCE I

A spicier spaghetti sauce for those who like some bite.

One 26-ounce jar spicy red pepper pasta sauce
One 2.25-ounce can sliced black olives, drained
1 tablespoon capers, drained

Heat all of the ingredients in a saucepan over medium heat. Simmer for about 5 minutes. Pour over pasta and toss.

Serves 6

PUTTANESCA SAUCE II

One 29-ounce can tomato puree
One 29-ounce can diced tomatoes, drained
1 teaspoon dried basil
3/4 teaspoon garlic powder
1/2 teaspoon cayenne pepper (or to taste)
1/2 teaspoon salt
1/2 teaspoon onion powder
One 2.25-ounce can sliced black olives, drained
1 tablespoon capers, drained

Heat all of the ingredients in a saucepan over medium heat. Simmer for about 5 minutes. Pour over pasta and toss.

Serves 6

ENCHILADA SAUCE

If you don't have a can of enchilada sauce on hand, you can easily make it up yourself with tomato sauce and a few spices. Add more cayenne pepper if you like it really hot.

One 15-ounce can tomato sauce
1 teaspoon sugar
½ teaspoon garlic powder
½ teaspoon onion powder
½ teaspoon chili powder
½ teaspoon dried cilantro
¼ teaspoon ground cumin
⅛ to ¼ teaspoon cayenne pepper (optional)

Mix all of the ingredients together. May be heated or served at once.

Makes about 1¾ cups

RANCH DRESSING

I love ranch dressing, but I don't buy it because it's either loaded with fat or, if it's low-fat, loaded with salt. Besides, I usually find it upside down in the fridge with a past-due expiration date. Since I keep sour cream on hand for many recipes, I find it's easy to whip up only when I need it. And using low- or nonfat sour cream brings down calories and fat, if you're counting.

½ cup sour cream (or yogurt, which will be tarter)
¼ cup evaporated or whole milk
½ teaspoon onion powder
½ teaspoon garlic powder
¼ teaspoon salt
⅛ teaspoon dried parsley

Combine all of the ingredients in a small bowl, stirring until well blended.

Makes about ⅔ cup

WALNUT CREAM DRESSING

This is a rich dressing that tastes like it requires far more work than it does. I've paired it with my Pear, Hearts of Palm, and Brie Salad (page 44), but it would be great on a number of different dishes that include fruits or vegetables and cheese.

1 cup heavy cream or whipping cream
1/4 cup finely chopped walnuts
2 tablespoons rice vinegar
2 teaspoons prepared horseradish

In a small to medium bowl, whisk together all of the ingredients.

Makes 1 1/4 cups

CAESAR SALAD DRESSING

I've trimmed down the amount of work required to make this dressing so that you can have Caesar salad more often at home.

½ cup olive oil
2 tablespoons bottled lemon juice
2 anchovy fillets from a 2-ounce tin, chopped fine or mashed
½ teaspoon garlic powder
¼ teaspoon dry mustard
½ cup real shredded Parmesan cheese (not powdered)

Whisk together the oil, lemon juice, anchovies, garlic powder, and mustard. Add the Parmesan cheese when you toss the salad and dressing.

Makes ⅔ cup

LEMONY VINAIGRETTE

Citrus juice adds a fresh twist to everyday vinaigrette.

1/4 cup olive oil
1 1/2 tablespoons rice vinegar
1/2 tablespoon bottled lemon juice
1/8 teaspoon dry mustard
1/8 teaspoon garlic powder
1/8 teaspoon onion powder

Combine all of the ingredients and either whisk in a bowl or shake in a lidded container until blended and thickened.

Makes 1/3 cup

CREAMY LIME DRESSING

Great on a summery salad or spring vegetables. This makes enough for two servings and can easily be doubled, tripled, etc.

3 tablespoons bottled lime juice
1 tablespoon salad oil
2 teaspoons sour cream
1 teaspoon sugar
½ teaspoon ground cumin
¼ teaspoon green Tabasco sauce (optional)

Combine all of the ingredients and whisk until well blended. Pour over salad.

Makes ¼ cup

LIME-MINT DRESSING

I've used this with my Chickpea and Orange Salad (page 35), but it would be great on any summery Asian- or Mexican-style salad. The recipe can easily be doubled.

1/4 cup olive oil
3 tablespoons bottled lime juice
1 teaspoon sugar
1 teaspoon dried mint

Whisk all of the ingredients together until they're well combined. Let stand for 5 minutes.

Makes 1/3 cup

BALSAMIC VINAIGRETTE

What could be simpler?

1/2 cup oil
1/3 cup balsamic vinegar

In a jar with a lid or a bowl, shake or whisk together the oil and vinegar.

Makes 3/4 cup

CRANBERRY BALSAMIC VINAIGRETTE

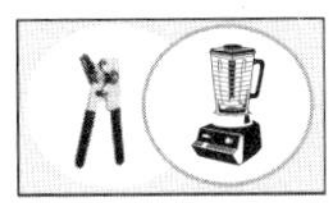

If you've got a little leftover cranberry sauce, try this wonderful vinaigrette.

¾ cup salad oil
¼ cup balsamic vinegar
¼ teaspoon salt
⅛ teaspoon ground black pepper
½ cup canned whole cranberry sauce

Combine all of the ingredients in a blender and process until smooth.

Makes 1 cup

SWEET ORANGE-BASIL SALAD DRESSING

This is virtually a fat-free salad dressing. Use it for shrimp salad or other green or vegetable salads.

1 recipe Sweet Orange-Basil Sauce (page 183)
1 to 2 tablespoons rice vinegar per cup of sauce

Make the Sweet Orange-Basil Sauce, then refrigerate until well chilled (about 2 hours). Before serving, whisk in the vinegar. The amount of vinegar you use depends on what type of salad you're making: Use less for a mild salad, such as shrimp, and more for something stronger, such as a salad with bell peppers and tomatoes. You can add the vinegar in amounts of sauce as large or small as you want, leaving the remaining sauce to use for heated dishes if you wish.

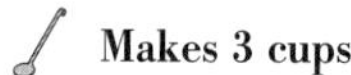

Makes 3 cups

Dipping Sauces and Relishes

SWEET HOT PLUM SAUCE

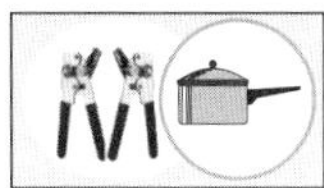

Sure, you can buy jars of plum sauce, but I always like knowing exactly what goes into my condiments. Serve on pork, duck, or Asian dishes.

Five 4-ounce jars plum-with-apple baby food
1 tablespoon bottled lemon juice
1 tablespoon rice vinegar
1 teaspoon soy sauce
½ teaspoon sugar
¼ teaspoon chili powder
¼ teaspoon garlic powder
¼ teaspoon onion powder
¼ teaspoon ground coriander
⅛ teaspoon allspice
⅛ teaspoon salt
Pinch cayenne pepper

In a saucepan, combine all of the ingredients. Stir and bring to a low boil. Simmer for 5 minutes; it's ready to serve when you are.

Makes 1½ cups

ROASTED RED PEPPER AND MANGO *COULIS*

A *coulis* is simply a puree put to work as a sauce. The color of this one is particularly vibrant—a beautiful shade of persimmon. I've paired it with Baked Polenta Wedges (page 116), but it's also terrific with chicken or fish. And it's so easy. If you tell people you made a roasted red pepper and mango *coulis*, it's going to sound like a far more challenging and exotic dish than it is. Eh, let 'em think that.

One 16- to 24-ounce jar marinated roasted (or sweet) **red peppers** (see Notes)
One 15-ounce can mangoes, drained (see Notes)
¼ teaspoon salt

With a fork, fish out enough red peppers to equal about 1½ cups (without liquid). Puree the peppers. If they don't make 1 cup of puree, add a couple more and process again. Continue until you have 1 cup of puree. (But really, 1½ cups of cut red peppers ought to equal 1 cup of puree.)

Drain the mangoes and puree. You should get about 1 cupful.

Combine the 1 cup of red pepper puree, ½ cup of mango puree, and salt. Puree them together again.

Makes 1½ cups

Notes: If you're using this with the Baked Polenta Wedges, consider chopping the remaining peppers into strips to drape across the polenta. Or use them on Jack cheese sandwiches or pizza.

Consider using the leftover mango to make a half batch of Mango Lassi (page 242), or use it as a sauce over ice cream.

MINT-YOGURT DIPPING SAUCE

Use this sauce with flavorful Mediterranean or Indian dishes. It's great with crudités.

½ cup plain yogurt
½ cup buttermilk or sour milk (Mix 1½ teaspoons of vinegar with enough milk to make ½ cup.)
1 tablespoon dried mint
½ teaspoon ground cumin
½ teaspoon bottled lime juice
½ teaspoon sugar

Whisk all of the ingredients in a small bowl until smooth.

Makes 1 cup

SPICY MINT DIPPING SAUCE

One 7-ounce can *salsa verde*
(green sauce)
2 tablespoons dried mint
1 tablespoon sugar

Combine all of the ingredients in a small bowl.

Makes a little more than 1 cup

SWEET PICKLE FISH SAUCE

Serve this homemade tartar sauce with fish on a moment's notice. (Some of my testers liked it as a sandwich spread as well.)

½ cup mayonnaise
2 tablespoons sweet pickle relish
2 teaspoons rice vinegar
¼ teaspoon garlic powder

Combine all of the ingredients in a bowl and stir.

Makes ⅔ cup

TOMATO-CORN RELISH

Serve this simple yet piquant relish with Southern- or Southwestern-style foods. It's also great on cornbread, baked polenta, tortillas, corn chips, burgers, steak, chicken, and fish.

One 14.5-ounce can diced tomatoes, drained
One 15-ounce can corn, drained
One 4-ounce can diced chilies, drained
3 tablespoons olive or other salad oil
2 tablespoons rice vinegar
1/8 teaspoon onion powder

In a medium bowl, combine the tomatoes, corn, and chilies. Whisk together the remaining ingredients and pour over the vegetables. Toss to coat.

You may serve this immediately or seal it in an airtight jar and let the flavors steep in the refrigerator for hours.

Makes 3 cups

Dessert Sauces

BROWN SUGAR–BOURBON SAUCE

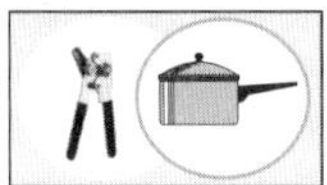

A quick and elegant sauce for grown-up desserts. Drizzle a bit on my Sweet Potato–Maple Pie (page 218) or on French vanilla ice cream, cheesecake, or sautéed bananas. Ladle a little on a dessert plate and adorn it with a slice of velvety dark chocolate cake. And though this recipe makes only 1 cup, a little of this sumptuous sauce goes a long, long way.

½ cup evaporated or whole milk
1 tablespoon butter
1 cup brown sugar
2 tablespoons bourbon

In a medium saucepan, combine the milk, butter, and brown sugar. Stir occasionally over medium heat, bringing it to a low boil. When the sugar is completely dissolved, add the bourbon and cook a minute more. Serve.

Makes 1 cup

BALSAMIC RASPBERRY SYRUP

The balsamic vinegar adds just the right amount of tang without calling attention to itself in this delicious dessert syrup. Spoon it over fruit, ice cream, pancakes, or waffles, or try it as a soda or coffee flavoring.

1 cup raspberry juice from a bottle, can, or box
1½ tablespoons cornstarch
½ cup sugar
3 tablespoons balsamic vinegar

In a medium saucepan, combine the raspberry juice with the cornstarch, whisking until completely dissolved. Add the sugar and balsamic vinegar, then heat. Bring to a boil, then lower the heat and cook at a low boil. Stir until thickened (just a few minutes). Remove from the heat. May be used immediately or cooled for later use.

Makes 1½ cups

BASIC RASPBERRY SAUCE

Fruit sauces are simple, flavorful, colorful additions to ice cream, cake, pie, cheesecake, waffles, pancakes, and even puddings. You can also experiment, adding flavorings such as vanilla, cinnamon, rum, maple, lemon, or mint.

One 16-ounce can raspberries
1 to 2 tablespoons cornstarch

Pour the raspberry juice into a small saucepan, reserving the berries in the can. Whisk the cornstarch into the berry juice until completely dissolved, then cook over medium-high heat, stirring very gently, until the mixture begins to boil. Reduce the heat and cook about 2 more minutes, until the sauce has thickened. Remove from the heat and add the berries, stirring gently. Let cool completely.

Makes 2 cups

VARIATIONS

BASIC BLUEBERRY SAUCE

Follow the instructions above, substituting one 16-ounce can of blueberries for the raspberries.

BASIC BLACKBERRY SAUCE

Follow the instructions above, substituting one 16-ounce can of blackberries for the raspberries.

BASIC STRAWBERRY SAUCE

Follow the instructions above, substituting one 16-ounce can of strawberries for the raspberries.

chapter 12

Desserts

PEACH SORBET

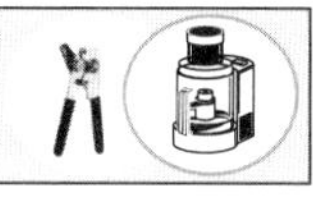

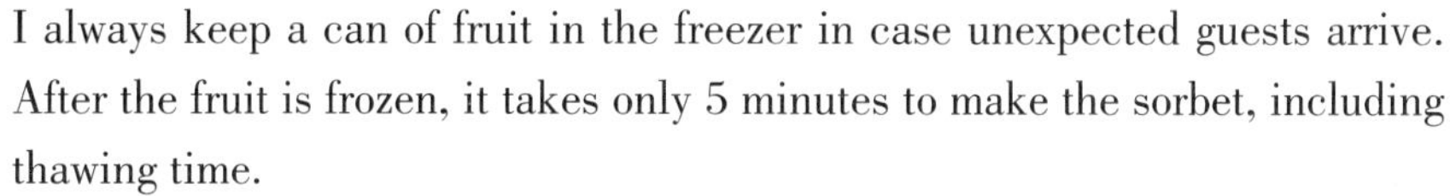

I always keep a can of fruit in the freezer in case unexpected guests arrive. After the fruit is frozen, it takes only 5 minutes to make the sorbet, including thawing time.

One 15-ounce can peaches
(Flavored peaches are okay.)
2 tablespoons bottled lemon juice

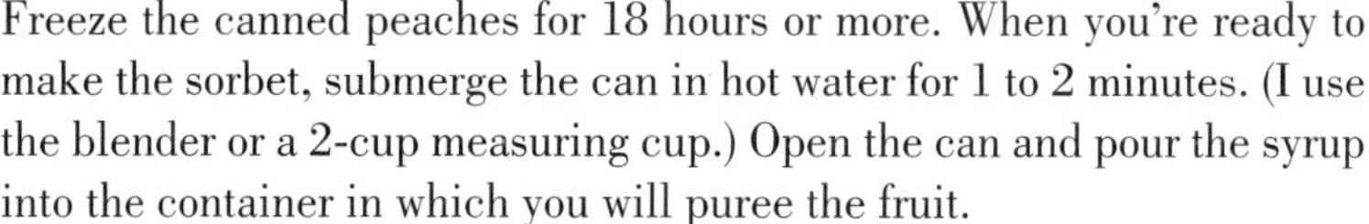

Freeze the canned peaches for 18 hours or more. When you're ready to make the sorbet, submerge the can in hot water for 1 to 2 minutes. (I use the blender or a 2-cup measuring cup.) Open the can and pour the syrup into the container in which you will puree the fruit.

Slice the frozen peaches into chunks. Add to the syrup. Add the lemon juice and puree until smooth.

Serve immediately or cover and freeze for up to 8 hours.

Serves 6

VARIATION

MANDARIN-LIME SORBET

Lime goes nicely with the mandarins and makes for a different kind of frozen treat. Follow the instructions above, using one 15-ounce can mandarin oranges, frozen, and 2 tablespoons bottled lime juice.

VARIATION

TROPICAL SORBET WITH RUM

The rum is, of course, optional. If you omit it, use 2 tablespoons of citrus juice instead of just 1 teaspoon. Follow the instructions above, using one 15-ounce can mixed fruit (preferably "tropical"), frozen, 1 teaspoon bottled lemon or lime juice, and 1 to 2 tablespoons rum.

VANILLA ICE CREAM WITH BRANDY-PLUM SAUCE

I love this. The fruity texture and tart flavor of the plums are tempered by the brandy, all of which complement the creamy sweet coldness of the ice cream.

One 16-ounce can plums in heavy syrup
¼ cup sugar
½ cup brandy
1 tablespoon cornstarch dissolved in a little cold water
Vanilla ice cream or frozen yogurt
Ground cinnamon (optional)

Remove plums from the can and set aside in a bowl, reserving the syrup. Heat the syrup and sugar over medium heat until the sugar dissolves. Add the brandy and stir. Add the dissolved cornstarch and bring the juice up to just boiling. Simmer and stir for a few minutes while the cornstarch thickens the sauce to a consistency like that of pancake syrup.

Serve warm with the plums over vanilla ice cream or frozen yogurt. If you like, dust the ice cream with a pinch of cinnamon first, then float the plums and brandy sauce around the ice cream.

Serves 6

CRÈME BRÛLÉE

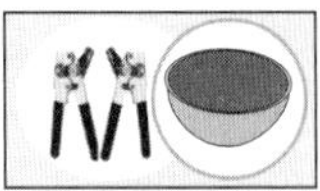

For a long time, I never attempted crème brûlée, because whenever I read that after you go to the trouble of making it you have to put the dishes in a pan with ice water before you put them in the oven, I sort of lost interest. But for this brûlée, the custard part takes about two minutes to make, plus a few minutes to set. Much easier. And if your milk has not been refrigerated, chill it in the freezer about 35 minutes first.

Two 12-ounce cans evaporated milk, chilled
Two 4-ounce or four-serving boxes instant vanilla pudding mix
½ teaspoon vanilla extract
3 tablespoons brown sugar for crust

In a medium mixing bowl, combine the milk, pudding mix, and vanilla. Beat with an electric beater (or whisk) according to the package instructions (about 2 minutes). Spoon into six ramekins or custard dishes and place them in the refrigerator. They will be soft-set in about 5 minutes, but chill for 15 minutes or more. (It's a good dessert to make ahead.)

When you're ready to serve, place your oven rack in the top position and turn on the broiler. Evenly sprinkle a thin layer of about ½ tablespoon of brown sugar over each custard, blanketing the entire top. (For even distribution, put the sugar through a sieve or sifter first. If you don't have a sifter, a coffee grinder does a good job, but you'll still have to use your fingers to distribute.)

Place the custards in a 13×9-inch pan, fill the pan with cold water about halfway up your ramekins, and throw a few ice cubes in the water. Place the pan on the top rack of the oven. After about a minute, watch them very carefully, keeping the oven door open if necessary. When they start to melt and bubble, take them out. The goal is to make the top crisp without scorching it. Mind the tops of the dishes, which can be very hot.

Serves 6

CHOCOLATE MOUSSE

Not only is this dessert easy, it's decadent. The evaporated milk gives the mousse an extra-rich and creamy texture. Plus, there are no raw eggs involved, so it's that much safer. You can also slim down this dessert substantially by using nonfat evaporated milk, sugar-free/fat-free pudding mix, and nonfat frozen whipped topping. It's all up to you. But you'll want to indulge in the full experience at least once.

If you don't keep a can of evaporated milk in the refrigerator, place it in the freezer for about 35 minutes or so before you make this dish. It needs to be cold.

One 12-ounce can evaporated milk, chilled
One 4-ounce or four-serving box instant chocolate fudge pudding mix
(Plain chocolate is tasty, too.)
1 cup frozen whipped topping, thawed

In a medium mixing bowl, combine the milk and pudding mix. Beat with an electric beater or process in a blender until thoroughly mixed. Fold in the whipped topping until blended. Spoon into five dessert dishes or keep it in one serving bowl. Place the mousse in the refrigerator; it will be soft-set after about 5 minutes and ready to eat, but it is also a good make-ahead dish.

Serves 5

SWEET POTATO–MAPLE PIE WITH BROWN SUGAR–BOURBON SAUCE

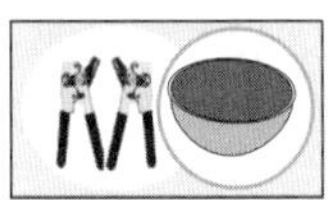

Rather than making an ordinary pumpkin pie, consider the sweet potato. It tastes very similar to pumpkin and provides many of the same great antioxidants. For the purists out there, I have been informed that there is indeed a difference between sweet potatoes and yams, but that it is acceptable to refer to yams as sweet potatoes. Which is why we're not calling it "yam pie." It just doesn't have the same ring to it.

¾ cup brown sugar
1 teaspoon ground cinnamon
½ teaspoon salt
¼ teaspoon ground ginger
¼ teaspoon ground nutmeg
¼ teaspoon ground cloves
2 eggs
One 29-ounce can yams/sweet potatoes in light syrup, drained and pureed
1½ teaspoons maple flavoring
One 12-ounce can evaporated milk
Two 9-inch ready-to-bake frozen piecrusts

Preheat the oven to 425°F.

In a small bowl, whisk together the brown sugar, cinnamon, salt, ginger, nutmeg, and cloves. In a medium- to large-sized mixing bowl, lightly beat the eggs. Add the pureed sweet potatoes to the eggs and blend. Stir in maple flavoring, then stir in the brown sugar mixture. Slowly add the milk, stirring or beating until smooth.

Pour the mixture into the piecrusts. Bake for 15 minutes, then reduce the heat to 350°F. Bake for another 40 to 50 minutes. The pies are done when a knife inserted into the center comes out clean. You may serve this pie warm, but many people like it chilled, like pumpkin pie. To chill, put it in the refrigerator for about 3 hours. Serve with Brown Sugar–Bourbon Sauce (recipe follows) if desired.

Makes 2 pies, serving 6 to 8 each

BROWN SUGAR–BOURBON SAUCE

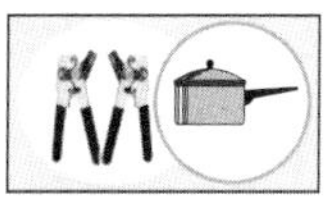

This is an easy sauce that makes sweet potato pie an even more luscious treat.

½ cup evaporated or whole milk
1 tablespoon butter
1 cup brown sugar
2 tablespoons bourbon

In a medium saucepan, combine the milk, butter, and brown sugar. Cook over medium heat, stirring occasionally, until it reaches a low boil. When the sugar is completely melted, add the bourbon and cook for a minute more. It's ready to serve, or you may let it cool and serve later.

Makes 1 cup

MAPLE-CARROT PUREE CAKE WITH CREAM CHEESE FROSTING

This is a simple cake, using pure vegetables from baby food, and the results are delicious. The cake will have a nice warm nutmeg color that looks lovely with the cream cheese frosting.

I've also given another frosting option—my grandma's Maple-Buttercream Frosting. It's delicious.

½ cup (1 stick) **butter, softened or even melted in the microwave if you don't mind a denser cake**
1½ cups light brown sugar
2 eggs
Three 4-ounce jars carrot baby food
¼ cup vegetable oil
2 teaspoons maple extract or flavoring
2 cups all-purpose flour
1 teaspoon salt
1 teaspoon baking powder
1 teaspoon ground cinnamon
½ teaspoon ground nutmeg
½ teaspoon ground cloves
¾ cup chopped nuts and/or ¾ cup chopped raisins or currants (optional)

Preheat the oven to 350°F. Lightly coat a 13×9-inch baking pan with oil or nonstick spray.

In a large bowl, cream the butter, sugar, and eggs together. Stir in the carrot baby food, vegetable oil, and maple flavoring.

In another, smaller bowl, whisk together the flour, salt, baking powder, cinnamon, nutmeg, and cloves. Add this to the first mixture, beating thoroughly. You should have a fairly stiff batter by now. If you're using nuts and/or fruit, add them now and stir well.

Pour the batter into the prepared pan and bake for 50 to 60 minutes, or until a toothpick inserted in the center comes out clean.

After cake cools, ice it with Cream Cheese Frosting (see below).

CREAM CHEESE FROSTING

8 ounces cream cheese or Neufchâtel cheese, softened
1 cup powdered sugar
1 teaspoon vanilla extract

If the cream cheese is not at room temperature, remove the wrapping and heat it in the microwave on high for about 15 seconds.

Beat the cream cheese, sugar, and vanilla until they attain a smooth, frosting consistency.

Makes enough to frost one 13×9-inch cake

VARIATION

MAPLE-CARROT PUREE CAKE II, WITH GRANDMA'S MAPLE-BUTTERCREAM FROSTING

Follow the instructions for Maple-Carrot Puree Cake, but substitute one 15-ounce can of drained, pureed carrots for the 3 jars of baby food. Frost with Maple-Buttercream Frosting (see below).

MAPLE-BUTTERCREAM FROSTING

2 cups powdered sugar
3 tablespoons vegetable shortening
3 tablespoons butter
¼ cup evaporated or whole milk
Pinch salt
1 teaspoon maple extract

In a large bowl, beat all of the ingredients until fluffy.

Makes enough to frost one 13×9-inch cake

PEACH CRISP

This is a snap to put together and makes a nice fruit dessert.

Two 15-ounce cans peaches, drained
1/3 cup chopped almonds
1/2 cup all-purpose flour
1/3 cup brown sugar
1/3 cup quick-cooking oats
1/4 teaspoon ground cinnamon
1/4 teaspoon ground ginger
1/3 cup butter, softened (6 tablespoons or 3/4 stick)

Preheat the oven to 425°F. Lightly coat an 8×8-inch dish with oil or nonstick spray. Place the peaches in the baking dish. In a small mixing bowl, combine the almonds, flour, sugar, oats, cinnamon, and ginger. Cut the butter into the flour mixture, blending it into a coarse consistency. Use your hands if you need to.

Sprinkle the mixture all over the peaches and bake for 15 to 20 minutes, or until the top is crisp and browning.

Serves 6

PINEAPPLE-GINGER UPSIDE-DOWN CAKE

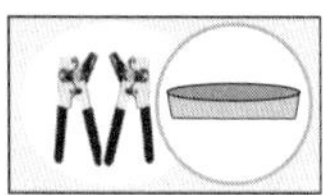

I couldn't very well have a Can Opener Gourmet™ cookbook without pineapple upside-down cake, could I? I've added a little ginger to update this sweet-scented classic.

One 8-ounce can crushed pineapple
2 tablespoons butter
½ cup brown sugar (packed)
1½ cups all-purpose flour
2½ teaspoons baking powder
2½ teaspoons ground ginger
¼ teaspoon salt
⅓ cup butter (6 tablespoons or ¾ stick), **at room temperature** (You can soften it in the microwave on high for about 10 seconds.)
¾ cup sugar
1 egg
2 teaspoons vanilla extract

Preheat the oven to 350°F. Have ready a 9-inch round cake pan.

Thoroughly drain the pineapple juice into a measuring cup (push to get ¼ cup). Melt the butter and pour it into the cake pan, tipping to distribute it evenly.

Sprinkle the brown sugar over the butter, then sprinkle the pineapple pieces as evenly as you can over the brown sugar (I use a fork to get the pieces out). Add enough water to the remaining pineapple juice to make ⅔ cup.

In a medium mixing bowl, whisk the flour, baking powder, ginger, and salt together. In another mixing bowl, cream the butter and sugar. Beat in the egg and vanilla. Add the flour mixture and pineapple juice mixture alternately in small batches and beat until well blended.

Pour the batter into the cake pan and bake for 35 to 40 minutes. Cake is done when the edges begin to brown and pull away from the pan or a wooden toothpick stuck ½ inch down in the center comes out clean. Invert onto a cake plate. (A few pieces of pineapple may stick; just scrape them right back onto the cake.)

 **Serves 8**

PINEAPPLE-GINGER UPSIDE-DOWN CAKE II

Here's an even faster way to make this cake—"cheating" with store-bought cake mix.

One 15-ounce can crushed pineapple
4 tablespoons butter
1 cup brown sugar (packed)
1 box white or yellow cake mix plus the ingredients it calls for
1 tablespoon plus 2 teaspoons ground ginger

Preheat the oven according to the cake mix directions and have ready a 13×9-inch cake pan.

Thoroughly drain the pineapple juice from the can into a measuring cup. Melt the butter and pour it into the cake pan. Tip the pan to distribute the butter evenly. Sprinkle the brown sugar evenly over the butter. Sprinkle the pineapple across the bottom of the pan.

Make the cake according to the package directions, but add ground ginger to the dry ingredients and stir. Then substitute pineapple juice for an equal amount of liquid called for in the mix. For instance, if it calls for ⅔ cup of water, add enough water to the reserved juice to make ⅔ cup.

When the batter is thoroughly mixed, pour it into the cake pan on top of the pineapple mixture. Bake according to the package directions. Invert onto a cake plate.

Serves 8

CHILLED RASPBERRIES IN BALSAMIC SYRUP

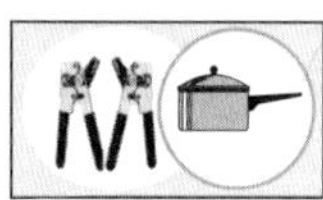

Though they're packed with a luscious tart-sweet flavor, raspberries out of the can don't look as colorful as fresh raspberries, which is why we disguise them a little here. Macerated and served in a champagne or other decorative glass full of balsamic syrup, they make a pretty, scrumptious, no-fat dessert. This recipe makes enough syrup to cover two cans of raspberries. If you make only one batch, consider using the remaining syrup for pancakes, waffles, or ice cream, or as a soda or coffee flavoring.

One 16-ounce can raspberries
1½ tablespoons cornstarch
½ cup sugar
3 tablespoons balsamic vinegar

Drain the raspberry juice into a measuring cup until you get 1 cup. You may still have a little draining to do after you get 1 cup, but it's not necessary to squeeze out every drop (they're delicate). Spoon the raspberries into three decorative cups or glasses. Set aside.

In a medium saucepan, combine the raspberry juice with the cornstarch, whisking until completely dissolved. Add the sugar and balsamic vinegar, then heat on medium-high. After the mixture comes to a boil, reduce the heat so it reaches a low boil. Stir until thickened (just a few minutes). Remove from the heat. Let cool for a minute or two if your raspberry glasses are not heatproof.

Spoon 3 tablespoons of syrup over each glass of berries. Chill for about 2 hours before serving.

Serves 3

CHEESECAKE WITH FRUIT SAUCE

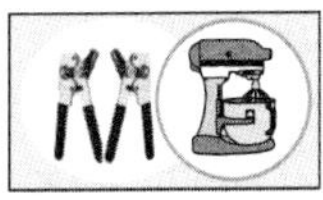

Cheesecake is one of the simplest desserts there is, yet its silky texture is nothing short of luxurious. Below the cheesecake recipe are a fruit sauce recipe with several variations and directions for using chocolate sauce. You can top cheesecake with just about anything and it will taste delicious, and if you use low-fat cream cheese, you get one-third less guilt.

Two 8-ounce packages cream cheese, at room temperature (If you don't want to wait, unwrap them and put them in the microwave on high for 10 to 15 seconds each.)
½ cup sugar
¾ teaspoon vanilla
2 eggs
1 ready-to-use graham cracker piecrust (Chocolate cookie crust is terrific for this, too!)

Preheat the oven to 350°F. In a medium mixing bowl, beat the cream cheese, sugar, and vanilla together until smooth. Add the eggs and beat until the entire mixture is well blended. Pour the batter into the pie crust and bake for about 40 minutes, until the middle is nearly set.

Cool and refrigerate for about three hours, or even overnight. Add selected topping just before serving.

Serves 6 to 8

Basic Raspberry Sauce

One 16-ounce can raspberries
1 to 2 tablespoons cornstarch

Pour the raspberry juice into a small saucepan, reserving the berries in the can. Whisk the cornstarch into the berry juice until completely dissolved, then cook over medium-high heat, stirring very gently, until the mixture begins to boil. Reduce the heat and cook about 2 more minutes, until the sauce has thickened. Remove from the heat and add the berries, stirring gently. Let cool completely.

Use this sauce to top cheesecake, ice cream, waffles, pancakes, or even chocolate cake.

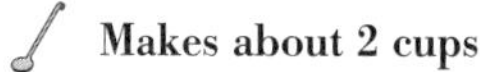

Makes about 2 cups

VARIATIONS

BLUEBERRY SAUCE

Follow the Basic Raspberry Sauce recipe, substituting one 16-ounce can of blueberries for the raspberries.

BLACKBERRY SAUCE

Follow the Basic Raspberry Sauce recipe, substituting one 16-ounce can of blackberries for the raspberries.

STRAWBERRY SAUCE

Follow the Basic Raspberry Sauce recipe, substituting one 16-ounce can of strawberries for the raspberries.

CHOCOLATE-TOPPED CHEESECAKE

Use a chocolate-crumb crust and store-bought chocolate syrup. Here are two easy ways to decorate:

Drizzle a stream of chocolate syrup back and forth across the chilled cheesecake, leaving minimal space between the lines. To serve, you may want to make a circle of syrup along the plate rim and draw a knife through it at regular intervals, just enough to make small points, then place a slice of cheesecake in the center.

Or make concentric circles of sauce on top of the cheesecake. Take a knife and draw lines starting from the center and continuing to the edge. You may alternate directions, too. You'll find it makes a lovely pattern.

LEMON BARS (WHEN YOU HAVE NO LEMONS)

It's great to be able to make lemon bars when you don't have fresh lemons available. Lemon extract is made with lemon oil, which is contained in the skin of the fruit. That's how we get the flavor of lemon pith/peel without the lemon. This crust is a little different—it has a little almond in it and is moister and more pielike than hard and flaky.

Crust

¼ cup ground almonds (Use a coffee grinder or food processor to turn slivered almonds or bits into a powder.)
½ cup sugar
1 cup (8 tablespoons or 1 stick) **butter, at room temperature** (You can heat it in the microwave oven on high for about 10 seconds.)
2 cups all-purpose flour

Filling

1½ cups sugar
¼ cup all-purpose flour
1 teaspoon baking powder
3 eggs
½ cup bottled lemon juice
1 teaspoon lemon extract
Powdered sugar (optional)

To make the crust:

Preheat the oven to 350°F. Lightly grease a 13×9-inch pan with butter or nonstick spray. Dust the bottom of the pan with the powdered almonds. (For those who have never done this with flour, simply pour the powder into the pan and then shake the pan around, tapping it until the powder is absorbed and coats the bottom of the pan in a light dust.)

In a mixing bowl, beat the sugar and butter until creamy. Stir in the flour until the batter has a doughy consistency. Press flat into the pan bottom. Bake for 10 to 15 minutes, until lightly golden. Remove and let cool for at least 10 minutes.

While the crust is cooling, make the filling:

In a mixing bowl, combine the sugar, flour, and baking powder; stir with a fork to blend. Add the eggs, lemon juice, and lemon extract. Beat by hand until smooth. Pour onto your crust. Bake for another 25 to 30 minutes, or until the center is set.

You may want to dust the top lightly with powdered sugar.

FUDGE IN A FLASH

This one's a lifesaver for holiday cooking, or for any other time you just want to pop a pan of fudge into the fridge. (Note: If you're trying to keep the trans fatty acids down, I've found brands of sweetened condensed milk that don't contain any. Just read the labels.)

16 ounces semisweet chocolate chips
(roughly 1½ 12-ounce packages, or about 3 cups' worth)
One 14-ounce can sweetened condensed milk
2 teaspoons vanilla extract

Lightly coat an 8×8-inch pan with oil or nonstick spray.

In a medium mixing bowl, combine the chocolate with the sweetened condensed milk. (It's a bit of a sticky mess, but it blends easily enough.) Microwave on high for 2 minutes. (You may also melt in a saucepan over low heat, stirring.) After 2 minutes, stir, and if the mixture hasn't completely melted, heat it a little while longer (try 10-second intervals). When completely melted, add the vanilla and blend.

Turn out the fudge into your pan, smoothing it as best you can. Cover with plastic wrap and put it in the refrigerator to chill. After about an hour it will be cooled enough to cut into squares.

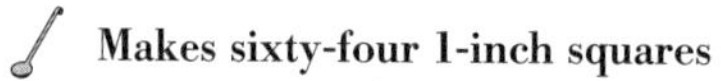
Makes sixty-four 1-inch squares

VARIATION

Add 1 cup of chopped nuts after adding the vanilla.

CHOCOLATE RUM BALLS

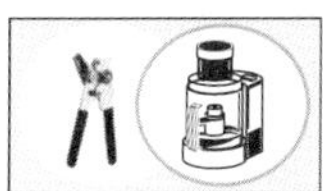

The great thing about this dessert is: no cooking! Simply roll the ingredients together and you've got the perfect addition to after-dinner coffee, afternoon tea, or coffee ice cream. They're also great to give as gifts during the holidays.

2 cups graham cracker crumbs
(You can find a box of them near the pudding section of your supermarket.)
2 tablespoons unsweetened cocoa powder
1 cup powdered sugar (plus more for rolling balls)
1/8 teaspoon salt
1/4 cup rum
1 1/2 tablespoons corn syrup, honey, or pancake syrup

Line a covered container with waxed paper; this is where you will store your completed rum balls.

Sift (or send through a processor or grinder) the graham cracker crumbs so that you have no big chunks of cracker. Place the crumbs in a large mixing bowl and add the cocoa powder. Sift the powdered sugar and add it to the crumb mixture. Add the salt. Whisk or stir with a fork so that everything gets blended.

Put the rum in a small cup, then add the syrup to it. Whisk together. Add it to the graham cracker mixture, then blend with your hands. (It doesn't seem like much liquid, but it goes a long way.) If, after squeezing and kneading it, you find it still isn't holding together, add a tiny bit of water, 1/2 teaspoon at a time.

Form the mixture into 1-inch balls, roll them in powdered sugar, and place them on the waxed paper. In the end, if you have crumbs left that did not get blended, add a tiny bit of water—just enough so that you can make balls out of them.

They can be eaten right away, but they're better after they've had a chance to "ripen" for about 12 hours or so.

Makes about 24

VARIATIONS

Add 1 cup of chopped nut meats (pecans, walnuts, almonds) to the mix before rolling them into balls.

Substitute brandy for the rum.

CHOCOLATE-COVERED ESPRESSO BEANS

These homemade candies lend a sweet but sophisticated note to ice cream or after-dinner coffee. They also make nice additions to gift baskets around the holidays. And they're so simple to make.

6 ounces semisweet chocolate chips
(about 1 cup)
4 to 5 tablespoons espresso beans

Slowly melt the chocolate in a saucepan or a double boiler over low heat, stirring as you do. You can also heat in a microwave oven on high for about a minute. The chips may keep their shape yet still be melted, which you won't know until you stir them. Test them periodically. When the chocolate is completely melted, spoon in the espresso beans and stir to coat.

Take two forks (short-tined forks such as salad forks work best) and lift several beans out of the chocolate, letting them drip a little if necessary. Take one fork and gently push off the beans one at a time onto a cookie sheet. If more than one bean comes off, it's okay—just separate them. Continue until all the beans are on the cookie sheet. (You may have extra chocolate after this and may wish to add a few more beans to correct this tragic situation.)

Let the beans dry completely before storing them in an airtight container, such as a decorative jar. Keep in mind that drying takes longer under hot and humid conditions, and in some cases you may want to dry them overnight.

Makes about 1 cup of candies

chapter

13

Drinks

CAFE VIENNA

It's amazing what a dash of spice can do for an ordinary cup of coffee.

Ground coffee
1 teaspoon ground cinnamon
Evaporated or whole milk
Sugar to taste

After placing your coffee in a filter, sprinkle the ground cinnamon over it, then brew as usual.

For each serving, pour about ⅔ mug coffee to ⅓ mug milk. Add 1 to 2 teaspoons of sugar (to taste) or 1 packet of sugar substitute.

Serves 2 to 3

BRAZILIAN COFFEE

If you like chocolate, you'll love this. It's very rich—perfect for a special after-dinner coffee. Or perhaps serve it as dessert with Chocolate Rum Balls (page 233).

1 ounce unsweetened baking chocolate or 3 tablespoons unsweetened cocoa powder plus 1 tablespoon vegetable or nut oil
1/4 cup sugar
1/8 teaspoon salt
1 cup evaporated or whole milk
1 1/2 cups strong hot coffee
1 teaspoon vanilla extract
1/2 teaspoon ground cinnamon

If you're using bar chocolate, melt it slowly in a saucepan. If you're using cocoa powder, put the oil in the saucepan first, then sprinkle the powder over it and stir. It will fully dissolve when it gets heated.

Add the sugar, salt, and 1 cup of water and heat to boiling, stirring as you do. When it's good and hot, lower the heat to medium and add the evaporated milk, coffee, vanilla, and cinnamon, stirring well. It's ready to serve when heated.

This coffee doesn't need whipped cream or steamed milk, but they would make it quite a decadent treat.

Serves 4

SODA CAFÉ

Ever feel like a more grown-up soda? This one's terrific as a dessert or an afternoon pick-me-up. It's delicious over vanilla ice cream as a coffee float. It's also a great way to use up extra coffee from the morning's brew. Lighten it to practically nothing by using nonfat evaporated milk and diet cola (and sugar substitute if sweetener is desired).

½ cup brewed coffee, cooled to room temperature
¼ cup carbonated cola beverage
2 tablespoons evaporated or whole milk
Ice cubes
1 teaspoon sugar or 1 packet sugar substitute (optional)

Combine the coffee, cola, and milk, then pour over the ice cubes. Sweeten if desired.

Serves 1

ICED BANANA LATTE

This makes a refreshing snack or special dessert drink. It's a nice complement to cookies, cake, or truffles. You can also add ice cream to make it a milk shake.

One 12-ounce can evaporated milk, or 1½ cups whole milk
One 4-ounce jar banana baby food
½ teaspoon vanilla extract
2 teaspoons sugar or 1 packet sugar substitute
¾ cup brewed coffee, cooled to room temperature
1 cup crushed ice

Process all of the ingredients together in a blender until you have a thick, frothy coffee drink.

Serves 4 to 6

VARIATION
ICED CHOCOLATE-BANANA LATTE

Follow the instructions above, but add 2 tablespoons of chocolate syrup.

STRAWBERRY FREEZE

I was so happy the first time I saw canned strawberries. I found them at a discount store, of all places, for about half the price one would find at a grocery store. This makes a great "slush" for kids or a natural base for daiquiris or other cocktails.

One 16-ounce can strawberries, drained
1 tablespoon sugar
2 teaspoons bottled lemon juice
1 cup crushed ice

Process all of the ingredients in a blender until smooth and frosty.

Makes about 2 cups

PEACH LASSI

Lassi is a traditional Indian beverage made with yogurt and often a fruit. Usually, that fruit is mango. One day I wanted to make mango lassi but had no mango. Peach is a pretty close cousin and worked just beautifully. This is a cool, refreshing, pleasantly tart peach drink that will probably become a favorite. In addition, yogurt has protein and beneficial bacteria we all need. So drink up!

One 15-ounce can peaches, drained
3 cups plain yogurt (low-fat is fine)
1/3 cup sugar (1/2 cup if you like it sweeter.)
2 cups crushed ice

Puree the peaches in blender. Add the yogurt and sugar and process until blended. Add the ice and process until smooth and frothy.

Makes 5 cups

VARIATION

MANGO LASSI

Follow the instructions above, but substitute one 15-ounce can of drained mangoes for the peaches.

SPICED APPLE SHAKE

Gravenstein applesauce makes a great base for this shake, since it's made from tart apples, whose flavor holds up better than other types for this drink. And since it's basically just fruit and yogurt, this drink works nicely as a dessert, a snack, or a morning beverage.

3 cups Gravenstein applesauce (see Note)
1 cup plain yogurt (Nonfat is okay.)
¼ cup sugar
½ teaspoon ground cinnamon
¼ teaspoon ground nutmeg
About 2 cups crushed ice

Combine applesauce and yogurt in a blender and process until blended. Add sugar, cinnamon, and nutmeg, processing again. Add ice and process until smooth.

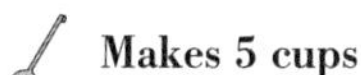

Makes 5 cups

Note: If you can't find Gravenstein or tart applesauce, add 1 tablespoon of bottled lemon juice to plain applesauce.

PUMPKIN PIE SHAKE

Pumpkin is absolutely loaded with beta-carotenes. And check the label—it's quite low in calories. This is a great way to get in those antioxidants any time of year. And if you want to cut back on fat, just use low-fat evaporated milk.

One 15-ounce can pumpkin
One 12-ounce can evaporated milk or 1½ cups milk
½ cup cold water
⅔ cup sugar
½ teaspoon ground cinnamon
¼ teaspoon ground nutmeg
¼ teaspoon ground ginger
⅛ teaspoon ground cloves
2 cups crushed ice

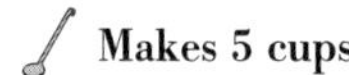

Combine pumpkin, milk, and water in a blender and process until smooth. Add sugar and spices and process again until well mixed. Add ice and process until smooth.

Makes 5 cups

HOT BRANDIED MILK

Here's a perfect drink to take the chill off a cold evening. Throw a few extra grains of nutmeg on top when you serve it. (Feel free to use nonfat evaporated milk if you want to take down the calories and fat a bit.)

One 12-ounce can evaporated milk
⅓ cup brandy
1 tablespoon sugar
Pinch ground nutmeg

Whisk together all of the ingredients plus ½ cup of water, then pour into two coffee mugs and heat in the microwave on high for about a minute each. (Or heat in a saucepan over medium heat until warm.) Sprinkle a few extra grains of nutmeg on top and serve.

COOKED EGGNOG

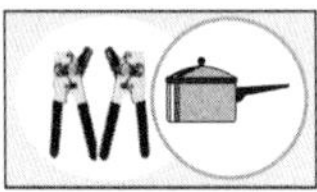

You can make this eggnog with or without alcohol. You might also consider using the egg whites to make meringue cookies later, or possibly as a wash for fresh-baked bread or pies (yeah, I know, but it could happen . . .).

One 12-ounce can evaporated milk, or 1½ cups whole milk
4 egg yolks
¼ cup sugar
½ teaspoon ground nutmeg
⅛ teaspoon ground cinnamon
Pinch salt
½ teaspoon vanilla extract
⅓ cup brandy, rum, or whiskey (optional)

In a medium-sized saucepan, whisk together the milk and egg yolks so that the yolks are completely blended. In a small cup, stir the sugar, nutmeg, cinnamon, and salt together, then combine with the milk and egg yolks. Add vanilla and cook, stirring, over medium high heat until thickened (about 5 minutes). Let cool.

If adding alcohol, do so just before serving. Garnish with a pinch of nutmeg.

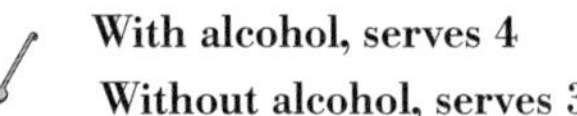

With alcohol, serves 4
Without alcohol, serves 3

LOW-SUGAR APPLE MARGARITAS

I had always made margaritas with Triple Sec and Crystal Light Lemonade, which cuts out a good deal of sugar from the drink. People actually stopped me at parties to ask how I made them because they were so tasty.

Then I decided to see what would happen if I substituted apple liqueur for the Triple Sec, which gives the drink its hint of orange. The apple worked beautifully. Now Apple Margaritas are always in demand at my get-togethers. You can easily double, triple, etc., to make larger batches.

While I don't usually mention brand names, I tried another apple schnapps brand and it didn't taste the same. So get the De Kuyper's.

1/4 cup tequila
1/4 cup De Kuyper's Sour Apple Schnapps
3/4 cup prepared Crystal Light Lemonade
1 cup crushed ice

Mix the tequila, schnapps, and lemonade. Pour over crushed ice. As an alternative, process all of the ingredients in a blender.

Serves 2

ORANGE BOURBON SOURS

Perfect for sipping out on the patio on a warm summer evening. (If you don't have orange juice made up, you can raid your kids' juice box stash.) The recipe is easily doubled, tripled, etc. Try these the next time you're thinking of margaritas.

One 8-ounce juice box, bottle, or can 100 percent orange juice
2 tablespoons plus 1 teaspoon bottled lemon juice
2 tablespoons sugar
¼ cup bourbon
1 cup crushed ice

Combine all of the ingredients and pour over crushed ice.

Serves 2

HOT TOMATO COCKTAILS

This could be Mexico's answer to the Bloody Mary. The tequila is optional—the tomato drink on its own is great-tasting and loaded with vitamins A and C.

One 28-ounce can or two 14.5-ounce cans diced tomatoes, *not* drained
One 8-ounce box or bottle orange juice
One 4-ounce can diced green chilies, drained
¼ cup bottled lime juice
2 teaspoons sugar
1 teaspoon hot pepper sauce (or to taste)
½ teaspoon salt
1½ to 2 cups tequila (optional)

Combine all of the ingredients except the tequila in a blender and process until smooth. Add the tequila, if using. You may also serve the tequila in separate shot glasses on the side.

Serves 8 to 10

appendix 1

Menu Suggestions

The following are menu suggestions, including some with themes. I hope you'll experiment!

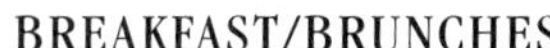

BREAKFAST/BRUNCHES

Banana Pancakes with Walnuts and Powdered Sugar
Café Vienna

Scrambled Eggs with Feta Cheese and Sliced Olives
Sautéed Breakfast Potatoes with Garlic and Onion

Overnight French Toast with Toasted Pecans and Maple Syrup
Hot Tea

Huevos Rancheros
Hot Tomato Cocktails

Peach or Mango Lassi

BRUNCH FOR A BUNCH

Raspberry-Pecan Croissants
Shrimp Quiche
Pineapple-Beet Salad
Creamed Potatoes and Onion

MEXICAN-THEMED LUNCH

Seviche with Corn Chips or Tortillas
À Santé Salad with Creamy Lime Dressing
Corn Pudding with Diced Chilies
Chicken Tacos with Mango Salsa
Low-Sugar Apple Margaritas

SOUTHWEST LUNCH

Baked Polenta Wedges with Tomato-Corn Relish
Cream of Red Bell Pepper Soup
Spicy Black Bean Cakes with Sour Cream and Salsa
Sun-Dried Tomato and Cheese Enchiladas
Iced Tea

GREEK DINNER

Hummus with Toasted Garlic Pita Wedges
Avgolemono—Greek Lemon Soup
Spinach and Feta Pastries
Greek Garlic Chicken
Lemon Rice
Lemon Bars

VEGETARIAN/ITALIAN DINNER

Parmesan, Pesto, and Sun-Dried Tomato Toasts
Italian Bean Soup
Tomato, Olive, and Feta Pasta
Baked Rosemary Loaves
Chianti

ITALIAN DINNER

Olive-Walnut Tapenade on Sliced Baguettes
Antipasto
Chicken Piccata
Green Beans and Red Pepper Salad
New Potatoes with Rosemary-Herb Butter
Blackberry Cheesecake

SUMMER DINING

Goat Cheese, Pine Nut, and Bacon Ball
Italian-Style Tomato Soup
Tuscan White Bean Salad
Penne with Chicken, Pine Nuts, and Tomato
Chilled Raspberries in Balsamic Syrup

Or

Sourdough Toasts with Baked Artichoke Dip
Pear, Hearts of Palm, and Brie Salad with
Walnut Cream Dressing
Stuffed Crab Shells with Parmesan Cheese Sauce
Green Beans with Butter and Garlic
Peach Sorbet

FALL DINING

Mushroom Pâté with Water Cracker Rounds
Cream of Asparagus Soup
Glazed Baby Onions
Beef Stroganoff Sauvignon
Chocolate Mousse

Or

Artichoke with Aioli
Corn Chowder with Roasted Red Peppers
Angel Hair Pasta with Shrimp and Lemon Cream Sauce
Minted Peas
Crème Brûlée

WINTER DINING

Baked Crab Cakes
Greens with Toasted Walnuts, Beets, and Gorgonzola
Asparagus with Lemon Oil and Pine Nuts
Turkey Tetrazzini
Lemon-Garlic Toast
Sweet Potato–Maple Pie with Brown Sugar–Bourbon Sauce

Or

Baked Spinach Balls with Yogurt Dip
Clam Chowder with Seasoned Oyster Crackers
Baked Salmon with White Wine and Parmesan
Creamy Green Beans and Potatoes
Chocolate Rum Balls with Brazilian Coffee

SPRING DINING

Spicy Peanut Dip and Crudités
Shrimp Salad with Sweet Orange-Basil Dressing
Carrots in Ginger-Lime Butter
Chicken Curry
Mandarin-Lime Sorbet

Or

Onion Dip with Crudités
Crab Bisque
Fusilli with Tuna and Lemon
Mushrooms Sautéed in White Wine
Pineapple-Ginger Upside-Down Cake

appendix

2

Stocking Your Pantry

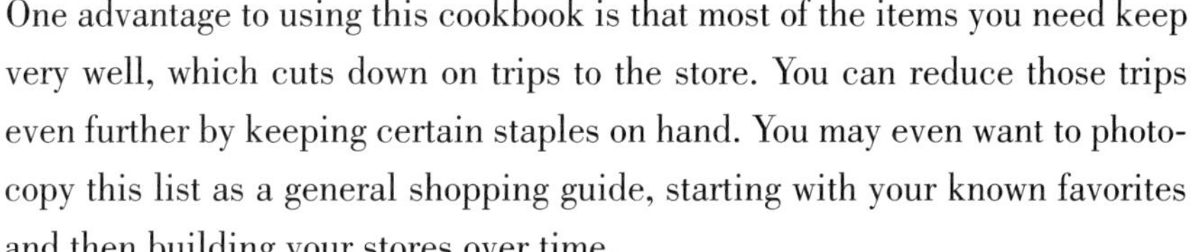

One advantage to using this cookbook is that most of the items you need keep very well, which cuts down on trips to the store. You can reduce those trips even further by keeping certain staples on hand. You may even want to photocopy this list as a general shopping guide, starting with your known favorites and then building your stores over time.

STANDARD CANNED ITEMS

Chicken
Chicken broth
Corn—whole kernel and cream-style
Cream of mushroom, chicken, or celery soup
Evaporated milk (12-ounce cans)
Green beans
Onions
Peaches
Pears
Potatoes, sliced and small round
Roast beef
Salmon
Sliced mushrooms (7-ounce cans)
Sliced black olives (2.25-ounce cans)
Sweet young peas

Tomatoes, crushed, diced, paste, puree, sauce
Tuna
Turkey

FOR SPECIAL OCCASIONS OR OCCASIONAL USE

Artichoke bottoms/hearts
Asparagus (white or green)
Baby food bananas
Baby food carrots
Baby food plums
Baby food butternut squash
Beans—black, pinto, small white, or cannellini
Beets
Capers
Carrots
Chilies, diced green and jalapeño
Crab
Garbanzo beans
Kidney beans
Mandarin oranges
Pesto sauce
Plums
Raspberries
Red bell peppers
Shrimp
Spinach
Sun-dried tomatoes
Sweetened condensed milk (12-ounce cans)

FLAVORINGS

Cocoa powder (unsweetened)
Horseradish
Lemon juice (bottled)
Lime juice (bottled)
Oils (olive, safflower, peanut, and/or soy)

Soy sauce
Vinegar
Wine (red, white, cream sherry)
Worcestershire sauce

OTHER ITEMS

Almonds
Baking powder
Baking soda
Butter
Cheese—Cheddar, Jack, real grated Parmesan (not powdered)
Corn syrup
Cornstarch
Eggs
Flour
Frozen piecrusts or pastry dough
Maple syrup
Mayonnaise
Pastas (fettuccine, linguine, penne, fusilli)
Peanut butter
Pine nuts
Raisins or currants
Rice
Sugar
Walnuts
Whipping cream

SPICES

Allspice
Basil
Bay leaf
Cayenne pepper
Celery salt
Chili powder
Cilantro flakes or ground coriander

Cinnamon (ground)
Cloves (ground)
Cumin (ground)
Curry powder
Dill
Garlic powder (*not* garlic salt)
Ginger
Marjoram
Mint leaves (dried)
Mustard powder
Nutmeg (ground)
Onion powder (*not* onion salt)
Oregano
Paprika
Parsley
Pepper
Rosemary
Sage
Salt
Tarragon
Thyme

Although the above is a suggested guide, you may really like something I didn't mention or you may detest something I did. Take spinach, for instance. I'm probably not the only one for whom it conjures memories of school hot lunches with the wet, seaweed-like mass nestled between the burned fish sticks and the hot molten apple compote. And let's not forget the smell. . . . But put that spinach into a Greek pastry and I'll happily eat it. Heck, I don't even remember where it came from. Which is sort of the point of all this. That, and you should eat the food you like and make the food how you like it.

appendix 3

Food and Flavoring Substitutions

1 tablespoon cornstarch	=	2 tablespoons all-purpose flour (for thickening purposes)
1 teaspoon baking powder	=	½ teaspoon cream of tartar, ¼ teaspoon baking soda, and ¼ teaspoon cornstarch
1 cup buttermilk	=	1 tablespoon lemon juice or vinegar plus enough milk to make 1 cup (Let it stand for 5 minutes before using.)
1 tablespoon onion powder or ¼ cup instant chopped onion	=	1 medium-sized onion, chopped (about ⅔ cup)
⅛ teaspoon garlic powder	=	1 clove garlic
1 teaspoon dry leafy herbs	=	1 tablespoon fresh herbs
½ teaspoon dehydrated lemon or orange peel	=	1 teaspoon grated orange or lemon peel
¾ cup cracker crumbs	=	1 cup bread crumbs

appendix 4

Measurements and Equivalents

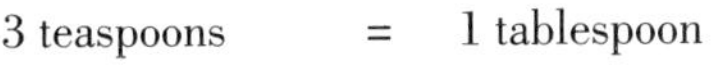
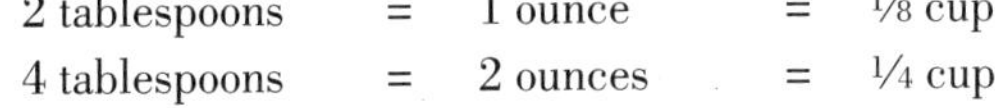

3 teaspoons	=	1 tablespoon				
2 tablespoons	=	1 ounce	=	⅛ cup		
4 tablespoons	=	2 ounces	=	¼ cup		
5⅓ tablespoons	=	3 ounces	=	⅓ cup		
8 tablespoons	=	4 ounces	=	½ cup		
10⅔ tablespoons	=	5 ounces	=	⅔ cup		
12 tablespoons	=	6 ounces	=	¾ cup		
16 tablespoons	=	8 ounces	=	1 cup		
16 ounces	=	2 cups	=	1 pint		
32 ounces	=	4 cups	=	2 pints	=	1 quart
128 ounces	=	16 cups	=	4 quarts	=	1 gallon
16 ounces	=	1 pound				

PANS AND DISHES

4-cup dish	=	9-inch pie plate, 8-inch cake pan, or 7×3-inch loaf pan
6-cup dish	=	9-inch cake pan, 10-inch pie plate, or 8×4-inch loaf pan
8-cup or 2-quart dish	=	8-inch square pan, 11×7-inch baking pan, or 9×5-inch loaf pan
10-cup dish	=	9-inch square pan, 15×10-inch jellyroll pan
12-cup or 3-quart dish	=	13×9×2-inch baking pan
16-cup dish or 4-quart dish	=	13×9×3-inch roasting pan

Index

Index

Index

Index

Index

Index

Index

Index

Index

Index

Index

Index

Index

Index